Guide to Night-Singing Insects of the Northeast

John Himmelman

Illustrations by Michael DiGiorgio

Line drawings by John Himmelman

Recordings by John Himmelman, Michael DiGiorgio, and the Walker Tape Library

CD narrated by Kate Davis

STACKPOLE BOOKS

0 11557 03548 3

Published by
STACKPOLE BOOKS
5067 Ritter Road
Mechanicsburg, PA 17055
www.stackpolebooks.com

Printed in China

10 9 8 7 6 5 4 3 2 1

First edition

Cover design by Tessa J. Sweigert

Library of Congress Cataloging-in-Publication Data

Himmelman, John.
Guide to Night-singing insects of the Northeast / John Himmelman ; illustrations by
Michael DiGiorgio ; line drawings by John Himmelman ; recordings by John Himmelman,
Michael DiGiorgio, and the Walker Tape Library ; CD narrated by Kate Davis. — 1st ed.
    p. cm.
  ISBN-13: 978-0-8117-3548-3
  ISBN-10: 0-8117-3548-6
  1. Katydids—Northeastern States. 2. Crickets—Northeastern States. I. Title.
  QL508.T4.H56 2009
  595.7'26—dc22
                                                                    2008029589

CONTENTS

ACKNOWLEDGMENTS

I have been working on this book for so long, I've had the time to elicit the help of a good number of people. First and foremost is the illustrator of this book, Michael DiGiorgio. I only hesitate to include him in the acknowledgments because this is his book too, and it feels as if I'm thanking someone for working on his own book. But I did the words, and he did the pictures, so I suppose I'm allowed the opportunity. Whenever I felt overwhelmed with this project, I would look at the sample paintings Mike worked up to sell this book and I'd get reinvigorated. To work on something like this with a friend, and to still be able to call him a friend afterward, is a great experience. His generosity with his single malt scotch didn't hurt, either.

Thomas J. Walker has been more than generous in looking over our species list early on in this project, and the information he makes public on his Web site is invaluable. He also provided us with several of the calls on the CD (they are listed in the back of the book). I visited a number of museums to study specimens; Jason Weintraub, at the Academy of Natural Sciences in Philadelphia, was the quintessential host, always clearing off an area for me to work, and helping me find my way around. When I needed photos I had forgotten to take, he took them for me and sent them via e-mail. Ray Pupedis, of the Peabody Museum of Natural History, was also very helpful.

I had put the call out to my naturalist friends to help me find some of the species we needed. Noble Proctor responded a number of times with species he and fellow naturalist Grit Ardwen managed to snatch up while in the field. He would meet me at a commuter lot to deliver the *goods*, something that had to look illicit to the passing cars. Carol Lemmon caught us our female Greater Angle-wing; Frank Gallo found our Treetop Bush Katydid (actually, it found him). He, along with Andy Brand and Bill and Cindi Kobak, joined us in hunting for Sphagnum Ground Crickets.

Since all refuges and most parks close at dark, I had to wangle my way into a lot of places after hours to find what I needed. The following people were very helpful in securing me permission: Sara Aicher of the Okeefenokee Swamp NWR, Georgia (who really went out of her way for me); Holly Holdsworth of Skidaway Island State Park, Georgia; Robert Cantin Jr. of Cedarville State Forest, Maryland; Amy Pimarolli of The Nature Conservancy in West Virginia; Brian Braudis of the E. B. Forsythe NWR in New Jersey; Tina Watson and Frank Polyak of the Bombay Hook NWR in Delaware; David Gumbart of The Nature Conservancy in Connecticut (who got us into the Beckley Bog).

Russell Galen, my agent, found a nice home for this book, and thanks must go to him! Thanks, too, to our editor, Mark Allison, who believed they might actually be able to sell a book on katydids and crickets. I need to thank my brother, Joe Himmelman, for my favorite LED headlamp—it has served me well on every outing.

My wife, Betsy, has become very good at looking interested in my katydid stories. I appreciate her efforts. And thanks, Kate Davis, for lending your wonderful vocal talents for the CD—no one says "Amblycorypha" the way you do!

Lastly, to all those people who saw some guy lurking in their neighborhood with headphones, shotgun mike, a bag of clinking glass jars, and a flashlight, that was me—sorry if I gave you a scare.

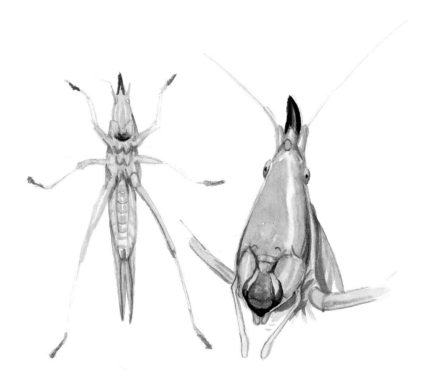

INTRODUCTION

*W*e all hear them. The true katydids scratching out their raspy chirps; the crickets staging their choruses of trills. They are the sounds of summer. They have replaced the calls of the Spring Peepers and Gray Tree Frogs, which have already seen to their nuptial duties. Come July, the night-singing insects begin to sing. By the end of summer, they've reached their crescendo, filling the soundscape of every yard, meadow, woodland, and tree-lined street. Most of us take these sounds for granted. They are just there. But some of us listen. We hear these songs and are grateful for our ability to appreciate what they do for us. Sometimes the sounds create an aural thread to our past, bringing us back to another time and place. Sometimes, we just enjoy that very moment and realize there's something going on outside our homes that may have little to do with us, but touches our senses.

But what are making those sounds? Though we can hear the katydids and crickets, we rarely get to see them. That cryptic ability allows them to survive. It's not easy being a bug. There are so many other creatures out to eat them that evolution had to come up with ways to usher them to adulthood. Katydids took the path of cryptic shape and coloration. They look like the leaves and grass upon which they live. Field and ground crickets blend with the soil and dead leaves on the ground, and spend most of their lives *under* things. They possess a rich diversity of forms that allow them to look like what they eat and the habitat in which they live.

While most guides deal with the eyes—what things look like—this one focuses on the eyes and ears. I don't know how this happened, but it appears *orthoptering* has arrived, and seemingly from out of nowhere! It helps that this new interest offers much of the satisfaction of the popular pastime of birding. For one, you have the songs, which can be used to identify the species. You also have the pleasing aesthetic quality of the insects that make those songs. Add to that the advantages of having fewer species to learn and the fact that your subjects tend to spend their entire life in one area.

It could be that the growing interest in butterflies and dragonflies got people thinking that insects had more to offer in terms of "the hunt." It is often the case that one interest leads to another. When you're out looking for one thing, it is impossible not to notice what else is around. That's what makes us naturalist types who we are. We're curious. One answer leads to three questions. One pretty bug makes us want to see another.

While a Swallowtail Butterfly gets noticed as you walk down a trail, however, a bush katydid is just one of the many leaves along the way.

The purpose of this book is to make those leaves jump out at you. You hear them; now it's time to put a face to the call. It's time to see them.

ON LEARNING ABOUT KATYDIDS AND CRICKETS

W hen I first set out to learn more about these insects, there were few references. Most of the books were nearly a century old and while the descriptions were full of vivid detail, they were written for other scientists. I had to learn a lot of new words to be able to make some sense of what I was reading. My most treasured guide is *Orthoptera of North-Eastern America* by Willis Stanley Blatchley, published in 1920. It's a big heavy tome with a black cover, appropriate in appearance and weight because it served as my "bible" for these insects for many years. I also greatly furthered the wear and tear on my already worn copy of Albert P. Morse's *Manual of the Orthoptera of New England*, also published in 1920.

Just to name a few more of the books that got me started: James Rehn's and Morgan Hebard's *Studies in American Tettigoniidae*, from 1914; William Beutenmuller's *Descriptive Catalogue of the Orthoptera Found within Fifty Miles of New York City*, in 1894; and Bentley B. Fulton's "oecanthinal" masterpiece, *The Tree Crickets of New York: Life History and Bionics*, put out in 1915.

The general insect guides, of which I've collected a good number, were of some help, but most of the katydids and crickets in my area were not very well covered.

Then I discovered Vickery and Kevan's *The Grasshoppers, Crickets, and Related Insects of Canada and Adjacent Regions*, published in 1985. This was a godsend! While it was still fairly technical, I found it easy to decipher and, what's more important, it covered most of the species of Orthoptera I was finding in Connecticut. Between this book and Vincent Dethier's *Crickets and Katydids, Concerts and Solos*, I had good descriptions of the calls of many of the species. My method of learning the songs is to catch the insects and bring them home. I find that watching them call helps imprint in my memory the song with the image of the caller. I've been doing this for about fifteen years.

And then there occurred a quantum leap in the information on this group of insects. Thomas Walker, from the University of Florida, created the Web site "Singing Insects of North America" (SINA). This has photos, maps, and recordings of most of the katydids and crickets of North America. He also makes available PDF files of scientific journals and specimen records. I found the latter to be very helpful when I was hunting down species for this book. This site continues to grow and is the most accessible and complete resource to the North American katydids and crickets.

I should also mention that my later efforts to learn insect songs were aided by a 1998 CD called *Songs of Crickets and Katydids of the Mid-Atlantic States*, by Steve Rannels, Wil Hershberger, and Joseph Dillon. It was nice to be able to pop the CD into my car stereo to immediately review what I'd just heard.

As I got to know these insects better, the urge to share my enjoyment of them grew. That's just human nature. When you enjoy something, you want others to enjoy it with you. It somehow enhances the experience. I did my best to remain cognizant of *how* I knew one species from another when I came across them in the field. While I discovered some new field marks, I also learned how to better utilize the techniques described in the books above.

In addition to the book and Web site resources, I made many trips to museums, most notably, the Academy of Natural Sciences in Philadelphia. Housed in this institution is the largest and most complete collection of Orthoptera in North America. I photographed, measured, and studied specimens of every species covered in this book. I also took copious notes on ranges. These were compared with the range maps on Thomas Walker's Web site and I found them to coincide quite well.

No book or museum can replace seeing the real things where they live. I have logged countless hours in the field from Florida to Maine. It started as a hobby, turned into an obsession, and then, when I decided to write a book, it became my job. As much fun as it's been, I am looking forward to this becoming a hobby again.

While my goal is to make identifying these insects possible for the layperson, I expect you will still be paying a few visits to the glossary. That said; learn the words below right away. They are vital to your understanding the descriptions in this book. While they are illustrated in the anatomy diagram, to navigate through the descriptions, you will need to be comfortable in your knowledge of their meaning.

Tegmina. Katydids and crickets have two pairs of wings. The tegmina are forewings, also known as upper or outer wings. They are usually thickened, distinctively veined, and in katydids are mostly opaque green or brown and are held tentlike over the abdomen. In crickets, they are transparent to translucent, sometimes opaque, and usually rest flat on the abdomen. Tegmina is plural for *tegmen*.

Stridulary organ/area. This is the area on the tegmina that contains the file and scraper for producing sound. It is located near the base and dorsal (top) section of the tegmina.

Hind wings. The two hind wings are located beneath the tegmina. They are either covered completely by the tegmina, or extend past their tips. Some katydids and crickets lack them entirely. These are the wings used for flight.

Pronotum. This is the plate that wraps around the top and sides of the thorax (the section of the body between the head and abdomen). The top of the pronotum is called the *disc*, or *pronotal disc*. The sides are called the *lateral lobes*.

Cerci. Cerci is plural for *cercus*. They are the pair of projections extending from the end of the abdomen. The shapes of the male cerci are unique in many species and can sometimes be used for identification.

Ovipositor. The elongated structure extending from the female's abdomen through which eggs are deposited.

Dorsal. Top—think of a shark's dorsal fin.

Ventral. Bottom.

Lateral. Side.

Dorsolateral. The area, often sharply or bluntly angled, between the dorsal (top) and lateral (side) surfaces. Many references are made to the dorsolateral ridges on the insect's pronotum.

KATYDID ANATOMY

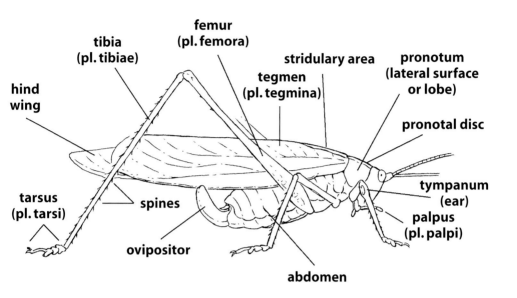

hind wing

tibia (pl. tibiae)

femur (pl. femora)

stridulary area

tegmen (pl. tegmina)

pronotum (lateral surface or lobe)

pronotal disc

tarsus (pl. tarsi)

spines

ovipositor

abdomen

tympanum (ear)

palpus (pl. palpi)

CRICKET ANATOMY

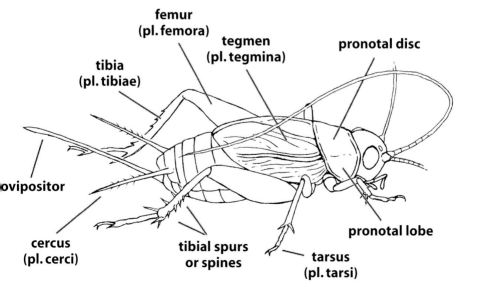

femur (pl. femora)

tegmen (pl. tegmina)

pronotal disc

tibia (pl. tibiae)

ovipositor

cercus (pl. cerci)

tibial spurs or spines

tarsus (pl. tarsi)

pronotal lobe

RANGE OF THIS BOOK

*M*y personal preference for field guides has always been for ones that cover a limited range. I find it easier to identify things when my choices are narrowed down. When we began this project, we were going to limit the range to New England. This would have forced us to leave out a number of nearby species, however, so we decided to add New York. Then, as long as we were adding New York, we figured we might as well go a little farther south to New Jersey. New Jersey added many species and we decided to end there before we had a guide to the entire eastern United States. We just would not have the time to cover all of those species. The western limit of this book falls along the Appalachian mountain range, although many species are found far west of this delineation.

The range information comes from museum collection records, personal experience, and the maps on Thomas Walker's Web site "Singing Insects of North America." While I was able to add a state or two here and there for some species, his maps added a lot more to my information than mine to his. I am indebted to him for all the work that went into it.

Bear in mind that the insects covered in the book never had a look at those range maps. Therefore they may very well be found outside of where they're expected. The range knowledge of the suborder of katydids and crickets has not enjoyed the benefit of layperson contribution as have some of the more widely observed insect groups. As more people look, unrecorded populations will surely turn up.

I should also mention that just because this is a guide to the Northeast, it does not mean you can't use it south of New Jersey. Forty-nine of the seventy-four species in this book are found south to Florida. Sixty-two of the species covered make it down to Georgia!

MEASUREMENTS

*M*easurements are included for all the species, even though for most of them, it is not very important to know an exact length. This is intended to give you an idea of the size of the insect in relation to others. In some genera, however, knowing if the insect is greater or less than a particular length can help you figure out what it is.

The measurements represent the length from the tip of the head to the tip of the wings or abdomen, whichever is longer. They were gathered from measurements taken of live insects and museum specimens. While many writers, and most entomologists, use millimeters, I chose inches or fractions thereof as the unit of measurement. Millimeters do give a more exact representation, but I felt that most people in the United States are still more comfortable with U.S. customary units.

FINDING KATYDIDS
AND CRICKETS

Since members of the three suborders are found in widely varied habitats, chances are any habitat you visit will host some form of katydid or cricket. I suppose the best way to handle this section is from the ground up.

Field and ground crickets will be beneath leaves, in the grass, or under logs and rocks. Most seek out somewhat damp environs, but there are those, such as the Gray Ground Cricket, that live in drier areas. Flipping logs is often fruitful, as is a method I call "stampeding." Stand with your feet pointing out, a la Charlie Chaplin, and slowly shuffle forward in the grass. Any crickets present will be driven ahead of you. This works even better if you are in the grass at the edge of a path or road. The crickets can be stampeded into an open area, where they can be scooped up in a jar.

Sweeping with a net can also be very productive. Sweep your net back and forth in both tall and short grasses and weeds. This will often result in a net full of leaves. As you look down into the net, tap the bottom to loosen up everything; the insects will then crawl into view.

I've also had some success with pitfall traps. This involves burying a jar in the dirt so that the lip is just a little lower than the surface. Put some fruit or dog food in the bottom. Cover it with a board and leave it overnight. You may end up with a number of different arthropods, including crickets.

The most enjoyable way to find crickets is to "prospect" for them. Get a white sheet and spread it out on the ground. Then grab handfuls of leaves and toss them on the sheet. Give it a shake and start removing the leaves to see what you've knocked loose.

Bush katydids, round-headed and meadow katydids, and tree crickets are found in tall grasses and sedges, weeds, and in low shrubs. They can be sought out day and night by following their call, or just by searching the plants. Tracking them by sound is accomplished by cupping your ears and turning your head back and forth and up and down, listening for the "sweet spot." This is the point where the sound seems the loudest. Slowly advance in that direction, stopping and listening along the way. If the insect suddenly stops calling, it may have seen or heard you, which means you could be getting close. Stop moving until it calls again, and then advance more slowly. Try sliding one foot out ahead of you; quietly set it in place, and then follow through with the rest of your body. Remember to keep changing your point of view too. Drop down to the level of the plants and search through the stems.

When searching at night, run your flashlight up and down the stalks of the plants. This makes it a little easier to find a break in the vertical patterns. I also find it helpful to set my sights for moving antennae, which tend to stand out a little better than the leaf-shaped insect you're looking for.

Check also the bark of trees and around your porch lights, which attract a number of the Orthoptera.

To actually catch the insect, I use any of a variety of jars or an empty cassette case. The latter works well for the smaller species and can be worked with one hand. The insect can then be transferred into a larger container if you wish to have it spend some time with you. A CD case works well too as long as it's not too thin.

I saw a design for a katydid catcher made by attaching two strainers to the end of a long pair of barbecue tongs. I never got around to making it myself, but I imagine it would work very well.

A number of the bush katydids and tree crickets are also found in the higher branches of the trees. So too are the angle-wings and true katydids. The arboreal tree crickets are often on the underside of the leaf; when they are calling, however, they move to the upper side or to a branch. Many chew a hole in the leaf and poke their head and tegmina through the top as they call.

The katydids will be on the leaf's upper surface. If you see one, and it's within reach, you can scoop it up with a long-handled net or with your bare hands. You can also use the pole of the net to rap the branches and shake the insects loose. Katydids and crickets tend to sail down on their wings and may land a dozen or so feet from where they were knocked loose, so keep a sharp eye out.

That leaves the katydids and tree crickets in the upper tree canopy. While they would usually be considered out of reach, these species just need to be at the top of the tree they're on. That means if you are in an area where the trees are relatively low, such as a fruit orchard, you may have access to them. I also seek out areas where there is new growth, as there may be "tree-toppers" settling for the tops of the young saplings. It may be worth your while to check the lower vegetation along a wooded area after a storm has blown through, since the wind and rain can knock them from the leaves.

THE ORDER ORTHOPTERA

*T*he Orthoptera encompass the grasshoppers, katydids, and crickets. Some entomologists include earwigs, walking sticks, mantids, termites, and roaches within this order. The "Orkin Man" and other pesticide companies that contain a version of the word orthoptera in their name surely consider roaches and earwigs Orthoptera. I'm happy to let the taxonomists fight that one out. The word Orthoptera comes from the Greek combination of "ortho," meaning "straight," and "ptera," meaning "wing." With regard to the grasshoppers, katydids, and crickets, the wings—most notably the outer wings, or *tegmina*—play a prominent role in their lives. These are the instruments with which they define territories, repel intruders, startle predators, and most importantly, call mates.

The Orthoptera are broken into two suborders, the Caelifera and the Ensifera. The former contains the grasshoppers. The latter contains the subjects of this book—katydids and crickets. Historically, a difference in ovipositor shape played a strong role in placing the members of these two groups within those suborders; however, they are more easily separated by the length of the antennae. Simply put, if the antennae are shorter than the length of the body, they are grasshoppers. If they are longer than the length of the body, they are katydids or crickets.* Some of the older literature calls them "short-horned" and "long-horned" grasshoppers, the *horns* referring to the antennae. It's an interesting way to remember the difference, but I find the use of the word "grasshopper" misleading.

Among the characteristics the two suborders share are long hind legs used for jumping. With few active defenses available to them, they often rely upon a quick thrust or series of them to carry them out of harm's way. Otherwise, to get to where they are going, they typically crawl. Hopping may get an insect to where it's going more quickly, but the action draws unwanted attention from predators. You'll probably notice that most of the grasshoppers you see while out and about were first spied as they were jumping out of your way. Hopping is also a waste of energy. Because most of these insects live among their food, there's rarely a big rush to get anywhere.

I mentioned that these insects have few active defenses available to them, but one that many do employ comes courtesy again of those long, powerful hind legs. The hind tibiae of many species are armed with sharp spines. A swift kick can effectively dispel certain aggressors.

While many Orthoptera have perfectly functional hind wings for flight, they are not generally considered "fliers," as are the Odonata (dragonflies and damselflies), Lepidoptera (moths and butterflies), and Diptera (flies and bees). Flying, like hopping, puts them in the more risky position of being seen by something that would eat them. That's not to say that these insects do not take advantage of their hind wings. The mass migrations of locusts are well known, as are their flying displays to attract a mate.

---

* One exception to this rule is the mole crickets, whose antennae are considerably shorter than their body.

Many species use flight as a matter of dispersal, or to hasten the arrival to a potential mate's perch or chamber. And there are cases when the food runs out and flying to a nearby source is the best way to go. It is best to think of them as "beeliners," whose flight takes them directly from point A to point B.

Members within the two suborders produce a different kind of sound from one another, via different methods. The Ensifera generally "stridulate" by rubbing their upper wings (tegmina) together. This produces a call that frequently has *pitch*—it's something you may be able to match with a hum. Insects that use sound to attract mates would be wasting their time if they lacked a way to hear them. The hearing organs, or *tympana*, of the Ensifera are located on the front tibiae.

Caelifera call by rubbing their inner femur against the outer surface of the upper wing. This produces a dry, pitchless call that can be compared to the sound of two pieces of sandpaper being rubbed together. Many also make a crackling sound, called *crepitation*, by rapidly opening their hind wings. Their tympana are located on the abdomen.

The last obvious difference between the two suborders is the preference of their calling period. In this regard, nearly all grasshoppers are diurnal. Most katydids and crickets are either both diurnal and nocturnal, or primarily nocturnal. This would explain the presence of long antennae in the katydids and crickets. Insects active at night benefit from the ability to supplement their eyesight with sensory receptors that function in the absence of light. Well-developed antennae play that role.

THE SUBORDER ENSIFERA

*T*his book could have been called *The Night-Singing Ensifera of the Northeast.* Ensifera means "bearing a sword," and refers to the long ovipositors borne by many of the katydids. This trait was used to differentiate them from the relatively short ovipositors of grasshoppers. Within this book are descriptions of the subfamilies, genera, and species of three families within this suborder:

Family Tettigoniidae—Katydids
Family Gryllotalpidae—Mole Crickets
Family Gryllidae—True Crickets

It is important to note that the classifications I use in this book are not necessarily the same worldwide. For example, some entomologists consider the Oecanthinae (tree crickets) and Trigonidiinae (trigs) to be *families*, making them Oecanthi**dae** and Trigonidii**dae**. I treat them as *subfamilies* in this book. My source for this, and for all the species in this book, is the Orthoptera Species File. This is a full taxonomic information database of the world's Orthoptera. It is largely the work of members of The Orthopterists' Society.

I believe the classifications used in this book represent some of the more recent, and widespread, thoughts on the subject.

KATYDID AND CRICKET DESCRIPTIONS

*W*hat follows are descriptions of all the subfamilies and genera, and most of the species of the katydids and crickets in the northeastern United States. Each subfamily is described in more detail prior to the genus and individual descriptions. Key features used to identify species are italicized.

Family Tettigoniidae—Katydids
Subfamily Conocephalinae—Meadow Katydids
Subfamily Copiphorinae—Coneheads
Subfamily Phaneropterinae—False Katydids
Subfamily Pseudophyllinae—True Katydids
Subfamily Tettigoniinae—Shield-backed Katydids
Subfamily Meconematinae—Quiet Calling Katydids

Family Gryllotalpidae—Mole Crickets
Subfamily Gryllotalpinae—Mole Crickets

Family Gryllidae—True Crickets
Subfamily Gryllinae—Field Crickets and House Crickets
Subfamily Nemobiinae—Ground Crickets
Subfamily Eneopterinae—Bush Crickets
Subfamily Mogoplistinae—Scaly Crickets
Subfamily Oecanthinae—Tree Crickets
Subfamily Trigonidiinae—Trigs/Sword-bearing Crickets

THE KATYDIDS

Family Tettigoniidae

*E*arlier, I wrote about separating the grasshoppers from the katydids and crickets. Now we need to separate the katydids from the crickets. The katydids are in the family Tettigoniidae. They have well-developed, sound-producing tegmina, long hind legs for jumping, and long antennae. They typically resemble leaves, twigs, or other plant parts. Here in the Northeast, they are leaf and grass mimics. Their resemblance to leaves is due to the fact that they are usually off the ground among them. The tegmina are laterally flattened, somewhat leathery, and held tentlike over the body with the left tegmen overlapping the right tegmen. In crickets, the right tegmen overlaps the left tegmen. Since the comparison to the appearance of a leaf can be somewhat subjective, there is a more reliable Tettigoniidae feature to count on when separating them from crickets: the tarsi. Tarsi comprise individual segments at the end of the tibiae and form the "feet." Katydid tarsi are made up of four segments. Cricket tarsi are made up of three segments.

As the word ensifera suggests, the ovipositor can be swordlike, but a more consistent description would be somewhat long and laterally flattened. In crickets, the ovipositor tends to be needlelike. The bladelike ovipositors of katydids are designed to slice into a plant—the leaf, stem, bark, and fruit—to deposit eggs. Sometimes it's used to squeeze eggs into a nook or cranny, and a few just push their eggs in the soil. Those eggs can take over a year to hatch, quite a long stretch for an insect egg to develop. Most katydids overwinter in the egg stage.

The Tettigoniidae members are generally leaf-eaters, but also feed on grass, seeds, fruit, pollen, and other insects. Because the basic leaf and grass colors in the Northeast are green and brown, so too are most of our katydids.

Katydids are best known for the sounds they make. The males are the primary singers, but in many species, the females produce sound as well. Katydids call by rubbing together two specialized areas at the base of the tegmina. This stridulary organ, or stridulary area, is located behind the pronotal disc (dorsal surface of the pronotum). It is obvious to the eye as the square or triangular dorsally flattened area just before the wings begin to wrap laterally around the body. You can usually see heavy veins across the surface. To produce a call, the katydid opens and closes the tegmina, allowing the scraper on one wing to rub against the file on the other. The varying size, shape, and forms of the file and scraper help determine the pitch and sound. So, too, do the size, shape, and venation of the tegmina, which amplify the call. The songs are further modified by the speed and frequency at which the tegmina are opened and closed.

Most katydids make more than one sound. The *call* refers to the more sustained sound used to lure a mate. Shorter aggressive clicks, ticks, and chirps repel competition or startle predators. Males in many species will stridulate in unison with other males to create a chorus. This generates a wall of sound that carries farther than an individual call, thereby drawing females from more distant locales.

The female selects the male based upon something she liked about his song. She then comes up from behind him and crawls on top to receive a special package. Tettigoniidae males offer the females an extra incentive to mate with them. This is a meal, called a *spermatophylax*, left for the female to devour while she is being inseminated. The insemination occurs, however, after the two insects have separated. Upon coupling, the male places a *spermatophore* (sperm packet) on the tip of the female's abdomen. The spermatophylax is then secreted on top of that. While the female feeds on the spermatophylax, the spermatophore is releasing sperm into her *spermatheca*, the organ that stores the sperm.

This meal offered by the male can provide extra nutrients for the mother-to-be. In addition, it can keep her too preoccupied with the meal to mate with other katydids or to remove the spermatophore before the sperm is released. It is not uncommon to come across these recently mated females bearing the foamy sack on the abdominal tip.

Katydids develop through a process called incomplete or simple metamorphosis. There is no larval stage; instead, the nymphs leave the eggs as morphologically similar, but wingless, forms of the adult. They go through five or six molts before reaching the fertile and calling stage.

The katydids in our area begin to sing around early July to mid-July. While farther south there can be a couple generations a year, here in the Northeast, we typically get one generation. Their calls peak by late summer, and as the weather cools, they slowly taper off. The pitches drop and rhythms slow as the cold robs them of their vitality. They continue on until the first few frosts, usually making it into November.

Six Tettigoniidae subfamilies are found in the northeastern United States. All are covered in this book.

Meadow Katydids
Subfamily Conocephalinae

There are two genera falling within the Conocephalinae subfamily in the Northeast:

Conocephalus—Smaller Meadow Katydids
Orchelimum—Larger Meadow Katydids

Smaller Meadow Katydids—Genus *Conocephalus*

Conocephalus means "conical head," an attribute that is fairly noticeable in the species within this genus. They inhabit upland meadows and other grassy, weedy habitats. Calling begins early in the day, and most will call into the early evening. Their food consists of grass seeds, fruit, and flowers. They've also been known to catch other insects, such as caterpillars, to feed upon.

They are similar in form to the *Orchelimum*, or larger meadow katydids, but differ in a number of ways. For one, the smaller meadow katydids are, well, *smaller*. In fact, with a maximum length from head to wingtip of one inch, with the exception of the Drumming Katydid, they are the smallest members of the katydid family. Many older references describe these insects as "dainty." While I can certainly see that, the term belies the fact that despite their diminutive appearance, their success in life's struggles comes no easier to them than to some of the larger, more imposing looking insects.

Most species within this genus are fairly stout of body, long-legged, and have hind wings longer than the tegmina. Most in our area have tegmina and hind wings that fall short of the tip of the abdomen. Wing length, however, is variable in this group and should not be relied upon as a definitive field mark for a species. Many of the short-winged species produce long-winged individuals.

As far as color goes, they tend to be green and/or brown. Some species that are predominantly green will have brown morphs and vice versa. Males often have bright yellow cerci. As with wing length, color should rarely be used to separate the species, although some, as you will see, do have unique coloration.

So, what *can* one count on to tell one *Conocephalus* from another? Fortunately, the male cerci are uniquely shaped in each species and are therefore your most reliable field mark. So too is the ovipositor, which varies on the theme of long and straight. It is shaped for cutting into the grass stems in which the females insert their eggs. The differences in shape and length between the ovipositors, however, can sometimes be subtler, and it may be easier to identify some females by their association with the males.

Lastly, there are the calls of the smaller meadow katydids. They produce a variety of clicks, ticks, buzzes, and whirs. They call during the day and into the evening. The song is not overwhelmingly loud—more likely something you hear before you realize you're hearing it. With practice, a good ear can tell most of them apart.

These are the most accessible katydids. A walk through a meadow will send them jumping and flying short distances out of your way. Watch where they land and approach slowly; you should have little difficulty in getting a good look at one and watching it call.

Identifying Smaller Meadow Katydids

An important key to identifying the *Conocephalus* is in the shape of the male cerci, the two appendages extending from the top of the abdomen (see illustration). A representation of the left male cercus is shown next to the male and female illustration for each species. Note too the shape and length of the female's ovipositor.

MEADOW KATYDID CERCUS

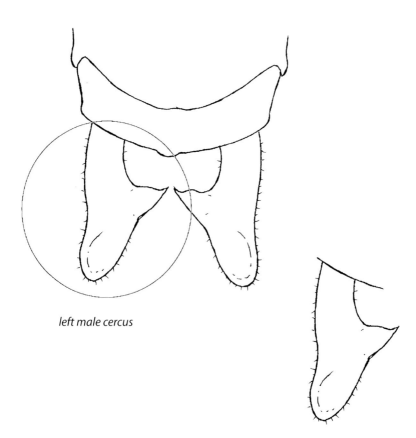

left male cercus

Range. Canada and south to Florida.

Habitat. Among the tall grasses and herbaceous vegetation in marshes and damp or dry meadows; roadside in tall weeds and grasses.

Size. $^3/_4$ to 1 inch

Body Features. As the common name suggests, the overall shape is slender. The tegmina are *long and extend in varying lengths beyond the tip of the abdomen.* The hind wings peek out just a few millimeters past the tegmina. The ventral edge of the hind femora lack spines.

Color. The sides of the body and head are apple green, as are the legs, although the tarsi and hind tibiae are usually infused with gray. The tegmina, pronotal disc, antennae, and top of head are typically reddish brown to umber, but in many individuals they are green. The brown on the top of the pronotum is often bordered by two white stripes. There is a yellowish wash on top of the abdomen.

Male Cerci. The tooth is stout and projects inward from about halfway down the inner surface.

Ovipositor. Long, straight, and angled upward. Color is green at the base and becomes reddish brown about two-thirds distance from the tip. It's about two-thirds the length of the femur. Because the length of the tegmina varies, the ovipositor ranges from falling short of their tips to greatly surpassing them.

Call. A series of soft, "locomotive-like" ticks, followed by a sustained, sputtery trill.

Similar Species. This is the only *Conocephalus* treated in this book with wings that typically *extend past the abdomen.* While there are no short-winged forms of this species, there are long-winged forms in the other species, so it is best to separate them by cerci shape.

Notes. This is the most common and widespread species throughout the United States, rivaled in numbers only by *C. brevipennis.* It's also one of the first to begin singing in the meadow. This could have played a role in its being one of the earliest named species of katydids. Swedish entomologist Charles DeGeer had some Pennsylvania specimens sent to him overseas. In 1773, he named it *Locusta fasciata.* The genus *Locusta* eventually evolved into *Xiphidium,* which means "swordlike," an obvious reference to the ovipositor. The Slender Meadow Katydid was known as *Xiphidium fasciatus* throughout the nineteenth century. Then in 1915, James Rehn and Morgan Hebart, thinking the shape of the head was a better indicator of the genus than the shape of the ovipositor, changed the genus to *Conocephalus,* and that's where it stayed.

Illustration on page 19.

Range. Maine and south to Florida.

Habitat. Among the tall grasses and herbaceous vegetation in marshes and damp or dry meadows; roadside in tall weeds and grasses.

Size. $^7/_{16}$ to $^3/_4$ inch

Body Features. Fairly stout for a *Conocephalus*. The tegmina in the males typically cover only three-quarters to seven-eighths of the abdomen. In females, the tegmina cover about two-thirds of the abdomen. Long-winged individuals do occur, where the tegmina extend at varying lengths beyond the tip of the abdomen. The ventral edges of the hind femora lack spines.

Color. The sides of the body and head are apple green, as are the legs, although the tarsi and hind tibiae are usually infused with gray. The sides of the pronotum and legs often have fine, black speckling. In males, the rear third and upper surface of the abdomen is pale yellow to deep orange. The tegmina, pronotal disc, antennae, and top of head are typically reddish brown to umber. The brown on the top of the pronotum is usually bordered by two white stripes.

Male Cerci. The tip is dorsally flattened, or concave. The tooth is stout, coming to a sharp point, and projects inward from about two-thirds the distance from the tip. They are the same color, pale yellow to deep orange, as the tip of the abdomen.

Ovipositor. Long, usually straight, sometimes curved slightly upward. The length is about equal to the length of the abdomen. Pale green at the base and turning reddish brown about four-fifths the distance from the tip. It's about four-fifths the length of the femur.

Call. A series of soft, liquid "tsicks" (one to five), followed by a brief, soft, buzzy trill.

Similar Species

Saltmarsh Meadow Katydid. Both species typically have wings that do not reach the tip of the abdomen. Saltmarsh Meadow Katydids, however, are restricted to salt marshes and tidal flats. Note differences in male cerci and ovipositor length.

Prairie Meadow Katydid, Conocephalus saltans *[not shown].* Another small, short-winged widespread species found in upland meadows throughout our range. See cercus drawing on page 16 for comparison—note the long, thin tooth compared with the *brevipennis* cercus. Call is a static buzz.

Notes. Widespread and common, the Short-winged Meadow Katydid often shares the same habitat with Slender Meadow Katydids and reaches maturity just a couple weeks later. Much of the literature on this species makes reference to William Morton Wheeler's 1890 account of this insect ovipositing on willow galls. The galls are created by a fly in the Cecidomyiidae family and apparently make as good an incubator for *brevipennis* eggs as they do the fly's.

Illustration on page 19.

Prairie Meadow Katydid (left male cercus)

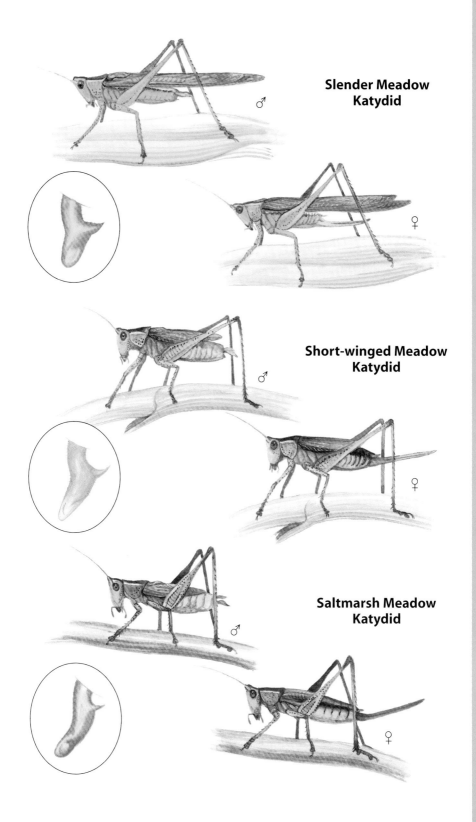

Slender Meadow Katydid

♂

♀

Short-winged Meadow Katydid

♂

♀

Saltmarsh Meadow Katydid

♂

♀

Range. Hugs the coast from Maine and south to Florida.

Habitat. Spartina grasses (hence the name *spartinae*) in salt marshes and tidal flats.

Size. $^7/_{16}$ to $^9/_{16}$ inch

Body Features. Slender; the tegmina in the males typically cover only two-thirds to four-fifths of the abdomen. In females, the tegmina cover about two-thirds to three-quarters of the abdomen. Ventral edges of hind femora have *one to four* spines.

Color. The sides of the body and head range from apple green to black. In males, the rear half of the abdomen is yellow to bright orange. In females, the abdomen is green on the sides and brown-black above. The female tegmina are translucent and infused with amber. The same for the males, except toward the tips, where they are *deep green*. The legs are green and heavily speckled with small, black dots. The tibiae are usually darker than the femora. A dark, brown-black stripe runs from the top of the head and ends about three-quarters of the way from the rear of the pronotal disc. The antennae are typically reddish brown to umber. The brown-black on the top of the pronotum is bordered by two whitish stripes.

Male Cerci. Long, slender with a small tooth about four-fifths the distance from the tip. The inner surface between tip and tooth has a convex bow. The tip is rounded. Near the base, it is the color of the abdomen (yellow to orange), but it starts turning green when it reaches the tooth.

Ovipositor. Straight, slightly projecting upward, and nearly equal to the length of the abdomen. Usually rust-colored.

Call. Very soft, high, sustained, rapid-sputtering buzz. A slight breeze rustling the grass can be enough to mask the sound to the human ear.

Similar Species

    Short-winged Meadow Katydid. See account on page 18.

Notes. These meadow katydids are very easy to catch. They only fly a few stalks ahead of your approach. Being meadow katydids, they immediately spin over to the other side of the stalk of grass, but they do not commit to the position as well as some of the other species. The males are a vivid mix of browns, greens, and orange, and worth having a close look at.

Illustration on page 19.

Black-sided Meadow Katydid — *Conocephalus nigropleurum*

Range. Northern New York, Pennsylvania, and a colony found in Ocean County, New Jersey.

Habitat. Grasses, sedges, and herbaceous plants in wetlands, also along the vegetated edges of lakes, ponds, and rivers, and salt water.

Size. $1/2$ to $5/8$ inch

Body Features. Somewhat stout. The tegmina in the males typically cover four-fifths of the abdomen. In females, the tegmina cover about two-thirds of the abdomen. Long-winged individuals are uncommon. The ventral edges of the hind femora have between one and five spines.

Color. The pronotum, tegmina, and legs are either yellow-brown or grass green. In both color forms the head is dark brown with a heavy band of ochre over the black eyes. A varying, usually lesser, amount of that same ochre borders the rest of the eye. The very top of the head is black between those bands of ochre. The upper and ventral areas of the abdomen are *shining black,* hence the name *nigropleurum,* meaning "black sides."

Male Cerci. Medium in length and width for this genus. A short tooth projects at a 180-degree angle from the inner edge (creating a straight line from the tip of the cercus to the tip of the tooth). The inner surface between tip and tooth has a very gentle concave bow. The tip is blunt, rounded, and somewhat flattened. In the green morph, it is green. In the yellow-brown morph, it is yellow-orange.

Ovipositor. Longer than the body, fairly straight, brown to black.

Call. Long phrases of buzzy whirs mixed with rapid ticking.

Similar Species. The shining black abdomen sets this species apart from the others.

Notes. I was looking for meadow katydids along a beach in New Jersey when a big, black Labrador retriever showed up from out of nowhere. I think something about the way I moved while stalking the insects grabbed his interest, and he joined my pursuit. He stayed a few feet in front of me, causing the insects to take flight. He never walked too far, too fast, or too close—he was the perfect katydid hunting dog! All I had to do was hang back and watch where the bugs landed. Most were Saltmarsh Meadow Katydids, but he also stirred up a number of Black-sided Meadow Katydids, which I did not think were in the area. These were the brown morph versions, and their yellow cerci glowed like little taillights in the setting sun. Something about that shiny black abdomen makes the rest of the colors on this insect stand out.

The dog's owner showed up and apologized for him. But I ended up thanking him and the dog for the help and companionship.

Illustration on page 23.

Straight-lanced Meadow Katydid   *Conocephalus strictus*

Range. Massachusetts and south to Georgia.

Habitat. Upland and dry grassy areas.

Size. $^1/_2$ to 1 inch

Body Features. Large, long-bodied, and somewhat slender. Tegmina are short; in males usually only half the length of the abdomen; in females, only about a quarter to one-third the abdomen length. Long-winged forms are rare. The ventral edges of the hind femora lack spines.

Color. Sides of head, pronotum, and abdomen are dark green. The femora are dark green and the tibiae and tarsi are often green infused with amber. The tegmina, upper surface of the abdomen, and pronotum are brown with some black. Top of head is brown to black. Eyes are green to amber.

Male Cerci. Long and tapered. Tip is pinched dorsally. The tooth projects inward about four-fifths the distance from the tip of the cercus. Color ranges from yellow-orange to amber.

Ovipositor. Very long—*much longer* than the length of the abdomen. It is fairly straight and angles upward. Yellow-brown at the base, becoming darker brown for most of its length toward the tip.

Call. Soft, buzzy, continuous whir.

Similar Species. While female Smaller Meadow Katydids are generally easier to identify by their association with the males, the very long ovipositor on this species makes it the other way around. The males, however, can still easily be separated by the cerci shape.

Notes. I don't know if the long ovipositor makes them easier to find, but I tend to come across more females than males. They are "droppers," often taking refuge in the lower tangles of the grass when disturbed. The large size makes you think *Orchelimum*, but the short wings set you straight.

Illustration on page 23.

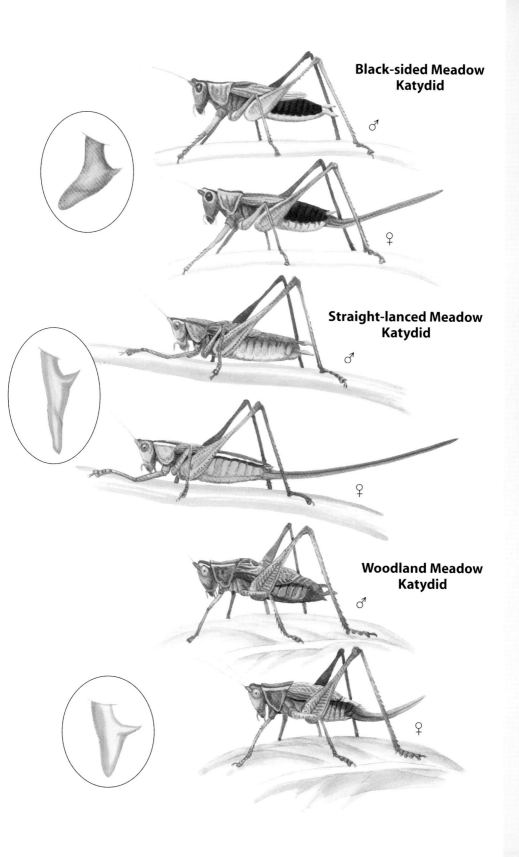

Black-sided Meadow Katydid

♂

♀

Straight-lanced Meadow Katydid

♂

♀

Woodland Meadow Katydid

♂

♀

Range. Connecticut and south to western Georgia.

Habitat. Woodland edges and old fields, among the woody and herbaceous vegetation well into autumn.

Size. $^1/_2$ to $^5/_8$ inch

Body Features. Stocky for this genus, like a small *Orchelimum*. In the males, the tegmina cover about two-thirds of the abdomen; in the females about one-half. The tips of the tegmina are broad and rounded. There is a fairly deep saddle behind the stridulating area. The ventral edges of the hind tibiae lack spines.

Color. Overall deep green and brown to black. The areas between the pale veins in the tegmina are filled with *black and brown,* giving it a very strong pattern. The sides of the abdomen range from deep green to black. The top of the abdomen, and the eyes, are often yellow-brown and are the palest areas on this insect. The tibiae and upper femora range from greenish brown to black. The antennae range from pale brown to black.

Male Cerci. Medium in length and width for this genus, with a thin tooth projecting inward at a slight angle about half the distance from the tip. The inner surface between tooth and abdomen has a gentle concave bow. The tip forms a blunt, narrow triangle. The color is pale brown, less bright than the male cerci of other meadow katydids in this group.

Ovipositor. Long, with a slight bow, causing it to curve upward.

Call. Short, gentle buzzes, given steadily, but with varying spaces between. It will also tick either independently, or prior to its trill. Calls mostly during the day, but into early evening.

Similar Species. The unique shape, colors, and patterns of this meadow katydid make it easy to separate from others.

Notes. I found this species, without realizing it, while recording crickets on an early autumn afternoon. When I got home later that day, I went through my recordings and heard this meadow katydid buzzing in the background. Fortunately, the site was only a short distance from my home and I immediately went back out to where I was earlier. Not only did I relocate *nemoralis* at the original site, but two more were calling at the edge of another meadow I passed on the way home.

Illustration on page 23.

Larger Meadow Katydids—Genus *Orchelimum*

In 1839, French entomologist J. G. Audinet-Serville coined the Greek word for this genus *Orchelimum*, which translates to "meadow dancer." While one doesn't necessarily think of katydids as dancers, perhaps he was referring to the maneuvers shared between the hunter and the hunted when the former attempts to observe one of these insects. The larger meadow katydids have the habit of shimmying to the direct opposite side of the stem from where you happen to be standing. If you go left, it shimmies right. You go right, it shimmies left, much like two dancers in the meadow.

The members of this genus are found in meadows, but their habitat tends to spring from wetter soil than that of the smaller meadow katydids. They are found in fens, marshes, and swamps, but also in upland meadows and other weedy areas. Calling begins early in the day and most will continue into the evening. Their food consists of grass seeds, fruit, and flowers. They also are predators, feeding on a wide variety of invertebrates, and at times, each other.

While they are similar in form to the smaller meadow katydids, they can most easily be separated by their larger size. The largest members of the smaller meadow katydids reach their maximum length at one inch. The smallest larger meadow katydids are $^7/_8$ inch and reach the length of $1^3/_4$ inches.

Most species within this genus are fairly stout of body, long-legged, and have hind wings longer than the tegmina. The majority in our area have tegmina and hind wings that extend beyond the tip of the abdomen. The stridulary area of the tegmina have a characteristic camel-like "double hump."

The cerci in males are often bright yellow, and the unique shape for each species makes it possible to identify them with confidence. The females lay their eggs in the stems of the vegetation. Their ovipositors tend to be somewhat curved, and their length and extent of curvature can also aid in identification. As with the smaller meadow katydids, however, it is easier to rely on their association with the more easy-to-identify males.

The calls of larger meadow katydids can be described as a static buzz, often accompanied by, or preceded by, a series of ticks. Because they are larger than the *Conocephalus*, their stridulary organs are larger and therefore produce a louder call.

Identifying Larger Meadow Katydids

An important key to identifying the *Orchelimum* is in the shape of the male cerci (see illustration on page 16). A representation of the left male cercus is shown next to the male and female illustration for each species. Note too the shape and length of the female's ovipositor.

Red-headed Meadow Katydid   *Orchelimum erythrocephalum*

Range. Eastern New York and south to Florida.

Habitat. Low vegetation in weedy fields, woodland edges, and roadside.

Size. 1 to 1^1/$_2$ inches

Body Features. Robust body with long, slender tegmina, bluntly rounded at the tip. The hind wings come to a slightly sharper point and usually extend past the tips. Males have the typical double "hump" in the stridulary area.

Color. Most noticeable is the *pale orange* to *cherry red* head. The sides of the pronotum and abdomen are deep green, as are the legs, except for the hind tibiae, which are brown-green. Tarsi are reddish brown. The dorsal surface of the abdomen is yellow to orange. The upper face of the pronotum and tegmina are yellow brown. There are usually two thin brown lateral stripes on the pronotal disc. The antennae are usually the color of the face.

Male Cerci. The cerci stand out, as they are yellow and in contrast with the green sides of the abdomen. The inner surface between the tip and tooth has a slight convex bow to it. The tip comes to a triangular peak, and the tooth, projecting inward from about half the length from the tip, resembles a hawk's beak.

Ovipositor. Curves upward, the tip usually falling short of the wing tips, but sometimes surpassing them (relation between tip and wing tips variable, and not a reliable indicator of species); greenish brown.

Call. A sharp, wet "tsick," followed by a buzzy burr. This is repeated continually in rapid sequence. As with most of the *Orchelimum*, they will sometimes just "tick." Calls day and night.

Similar Species. This is the only species covered in our area with a pink to red head. The call too is unique in that it is steady and interrupted regularly by a tick, as opposed to the others that seem to introduce their call with a series of ticks.

Notes. Sometimes you have to work very hard to catch a glimpse of the more beautiful creatures on this planet, and the challenge of the quest enhances the appreciation of that elusive species you seek. This species doesn't make you work very hard. If Red-headed Meadow Katydids are in the area, chances are you will be able to find them. They call early on in the day and into the night, loudly, and can be more forgiving of your approach than other *Orchelimum* katydids.

Illustration on page 27.

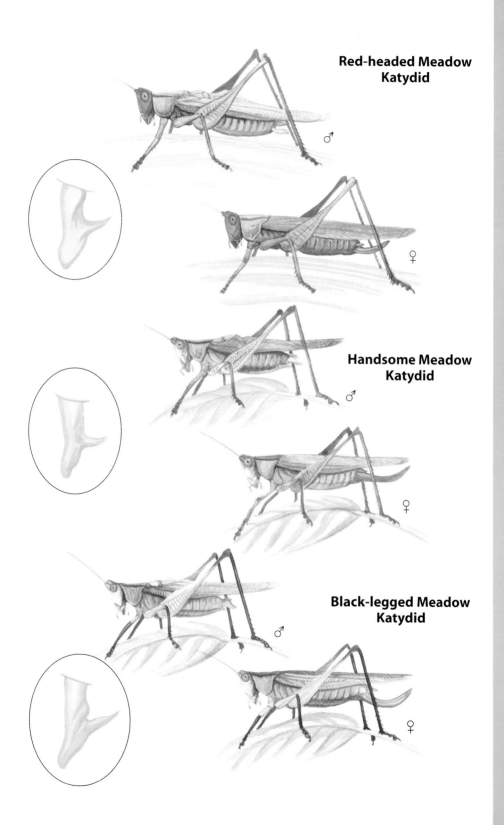

Red-headed Meadow Katydid

♂

♀

Handsome Meadow Katydid

♂

♀

Black-legged Meadow Katydid

♂

♀

Range. New Jersey and south to Florida.

Habitat. Meadows and weedy fields along the edges of ponds, streams, and other wetlands and watercourses.

Size. $^7/_8$ to 1 inch

Body Features. Robust body with long, slender tegmina, bluntly rounded at the tip. The hind wings come to a slightly sharper point and usually extend past the tips. Males have the typical double "hump" in the stridulary area.

Color. The face is a pale, buttery yellow and is bordered on the top of the head and rear of the face with deep maroon. The maroon extends into the yellow in a *broken web pattern.* Eyes are yellow to blue. The sides of the pronotum and abdomen are deep blue-green. Tegmina are blue-green, infused with brown. The leg colors are highly variable; femora range from yellow to green, and are peppered with small black dots; tibiae range from green to maroon, the hind tibiae often red-brown to black. The dorsal surface of the abdomen is usually brown. The upper face of the pronotum is brownish, with two thin brown lateral stripes, the outer edges bordered with white. The antennae range from pale yellow to black.

Male Cerci. The cerci stand out, as they are yellow and contrast with the green sides of the abdomen. The inner surface of the area between the tip and tooth, and the tooth and base, is fairly straight. The tooth projects inward from about half the length from the tip.

Ovipositor. Curves upward, the tip usually near the wing tips (relation between tip and wing tips variable, and not a reliable indicator of species); yellowish green and red.

Call. A couple quick "tsicks," or a short series of them, followed by a more sustained, buzzy trill. As with most of the *Orchelimum*, they will sometimes just "tick." Calls day and night.

Similar Species

Black-legged Meadow Katydid. This species is very closely related to the Handsome Meadow Katydid, and the two have been known to interbreed. The best way to tell the difference is by comparing the shapes of the male cerci. The femora of Black-legged Meadow Katydids are almost always black. Those of the Handsome Meadow Katydid can be very dark, but are more typically yellow to deep, dusky red.

Notes. I was in a field, recording calling Handsomes and had one so close that it was "spiking" my shotgun microphone. I was right on top of it, but could not find the actual insect. Judging from the sound coming through my headphones, the call was somehow bouncing off a tall stem of grass *six inches* in front of my face. How could this be? I stared and stared at that piece of grass and could not figure out how such a skinny surface could bounce a sound. It was getting frustrating.

Then I saw a little antenna peek out. I spun the grass in my fingertips, and there was the katydid. It was in front of my eyes the whole time, but was so adept at slipping to the direct opposite side of my face, it had remained nearly invisible.

Illustration on page 27.

Black-legged Meadow Katydid — *Orchelimum nigripes*

Range. Connecticut and south to Maryland.

Habitat. Meadows and weedy fields along the edges of ponds, rivers, and other wetlands and watercourses.

Size. $7/8$ to 1 inch

Body Features. Robust body with long, slender tegmina, bluntly rounded at the tip. The hind wings come to a slightly sharper point and usually extend past the tips. Males have the typical double "hump" in the stridulary area.

Color. The face is a pale whitish green and is bordered on the top of the head and rear of the face with deep brown-black. The brown-black extends into the paler face in a broken web pattern. Eyes are usually reddish. The sides of the pronotum and abdomen are deep blue-green. Tegmina are blue-green, infused with a little brown and yellow. The femora are yellow-orange, and are sometimes peppered with small black dots; upper areas of the hind femora are black. Tibiae are *black,* as the name of this insect suggests. The dorsal surface of the abdomen is usually brown. The upper face of the pronotum is brownish, with two thin brown lateral stripes, the outer edges sometimes bordered with white. The antennae range from pale yellow to black.

Male Cerci. The cerci stand out, as they are yellow and contrast with the green sides of the abdomen. The tip forms a quarter circle. The inner surface between the tip and tooth has a gentle bump. There is a strong bump by the tooth between the tooth and base. The tooth projects inward from about half the length from the tip.

Ovipositor. Curves upward, the tip usually near the wing tips (relation between tip and wing tips variable, and not a reliable indicator of species); yellowish green and red.

Call. A couple quick ticks, or a short series of them, followed by a more sustained, buzzy trill. As with most of the *Orchelimum*, they will sometimes just "tick." Calls day and night.

Similar Species

    Handsome Meadow Katydid. See account on page 28.

Notes. This katydid took me for a fun ride. I found a large colony of them at a state park along the Connecticut River. They were not *supposed* to be there. The closest population in the East was supposed to be in Maryland. And to the west, there were no records I knew of beyond Pennsylvania. This proves once again that there is much room out there for discovery in this group. There are lots of people looking for birds, so we have a good idea of where they should be, and when they should be there. The same goes for butterflies, and it seems we're getting a good handle on the Odonata. But who's out there looking for crickets and katydids? Hopefully, now you are.

Illustration on page 27.

Common Meadow Katydid   *Orchelimum vulgare*

Range. Maine and south to Georgia.

Habitat. Upland meadows and weedy fields; fens.

Size. $^7/_8$ to $1^1/_4$ inches

Body Features. Heavy-bodied with long, slender tegmina, bluntly rounded at the tip. The hind wings come to a slightly sharper point and usually extend past the tips. Males have the typical double "hump" in the stridulary area.

Color. The face and head are green; top of head brown. Eyes are yellow to orange. The sides of the pronotum, abdomen, and femora are apple green. Tegmina are green, infused with yellowish brown. The legs are yellow to green, except for the hind tibiae, which are a darker brown-green. The dorsal surface of the abdomen is yellow to brown, or both. The upper face of the pronotum is brownish, with two thin lateral brown stripes, the outer edges bordered with white. The antennae are pale to dark brown.

Male Cerci. The cerci stand out, as they are yellow and contrast with the green sides of the abdomen. The tip is roundly triangular. The inner surface of the area between the tip and tooth has a gentle bump. There is a very weak bump by the tooth between the tooth and base. The tooth projects inward from about half the distance from the cercus tip and hooks strongly at the tip.

Ovipositor. *Curves weakly upward.* The tip usually falls short of the wing tips, but can also extend beyond them (relation between tip and wing tips variable, and not a reliable indicator of species); yellow-brown.

Call. Many "tsicks," followed by a sustained buzz that grows louder toward the end. As with most of the *Orchelimum*, they will sometimes just "tick." Calls day and night.

Similar Species

Gladiator Meadow Katydid. This species is closely related and is best separated by the difference in the shape of the male cerci and the female's ovipositor. The upper and lower edges of the ovipositor in Common Meadow Katydids are curved; in Gladiator Meadow Katydids, the upper edge is nearly straight. Also, the two "humps" in the tegmina are more pronounced in this species. Many Gladiators have a dark eclipse in the front of the eye, whereas Common Meadow Katydids do not. Also, in the Common Meadow Katydid, there is a deep, concave depression in the rear edge along the sides of the pronotum. In the Gladiator, there is hardly any depression.

Lesser Pine Katydid, Orchelimum minor *[not shown].* This species is similar in color—deep green with brownish green tegmina. The tibiae, however, are orange-brown. They inhabit conifers and are found from Long Island, New York, south to Florida. Their call is a series of short, bubbly sputters.

Notes. When I do find these individuals, they're often sharing the meadow with Gladiator Meadow Katydids. While they do the typical "meadow dance" when approached, their hiding seems more of an afterthought when compared with the other *Orchelimum* species. Like other meadow katydids, they will not pass up the opportunity to eat other insects in the meadow.

Illustration on page 31.

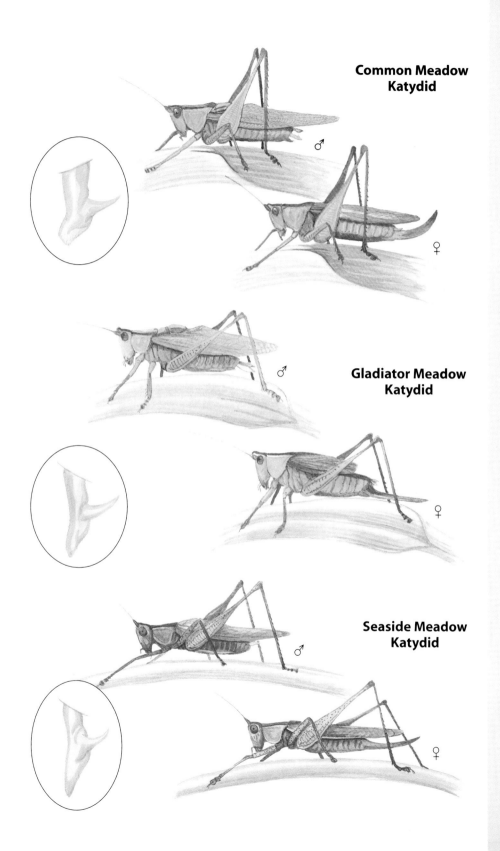

Common Meadow Katydid

♂

♀

Gladiator Meadow Katydid

♂

♀

Seaside Meadow Katydid

♂

♀

Gladiator Meadow Katydid   *Orchelimum gladiator*

Range. Maine and south to Maryland.

Habitat. Wet and dry meadows and weedy fields.

Size. $^7/_8$ to $^{13}/_{16}$ inch

Body Features. Very heavy-bodied with tegmina somewhat broad for this genus, and bluntly rounded at the tip. The hind wings usually do not extend past the tips. Males have the typical "humps" in the stridulary area, but a bit more pronounced in this species.

Color. The face and head are green; top of head brown. Eyes are yellow to deep orange, and often have a *dark "eclipsed" area* toward the front. The sides of the pronotum, abdomen, and femora are apple green. Tegmina are green, infused with yellowish brown. The legs are green; tibiae sometimes brownish. The dorsal surface of the abdomen is yellow to brown, or both. The upper face of the pronotum is brownish, with two thin lateral brown stripes, the outer edges bordered with white. The antennae are pale to dark brown.

Male Cerci. The cerci stand out, as they are yellow and contrast with the green sides of the abdomen. The tip is triangular. The inner surface of the area between the tip and tooth has a gentle bump. The area between the tooth and base is fairly straight. The tooth is long and thin, projecting inward from about half the distance from the tip.

Ovipositor. Heavy and *fairly straight* along the dorsal edge, curved below, and usually extends beyond wing tips (relation between tip and wing tips variable, and not a reliable indicator of species); yellow-brown.

Call. Several "tsicks," followed by a sustained, soft whir that grows louder toward the end. As with most of the *Orchelimum*, they will sometimes just "tick." Calls day and night.

Similar Species

   Common Meadow Katydid. See account on page 30.

Notes. This meadow katydid is a powerful-looking creature and is well named. It is, however, very wary and good at hiding. Because they choose hiding behind a grass stem over flying away, if you keep your eye on the stalk where you saw one, you can walk right up to the insect. It will continue to move to the opposite side of the stem, but you can trick it into revealing itself for a good look or photograph. Keeping your face and body still, slowly move your hand in a wide arc around to the side where the katydid is hiding. The katydid will usually attempt to hide from your hand and will shimmy into view.

Illustration on page 31.

Seaside Meadow Katydid   *Orchelimum fidicinium*

Range. Hugs the coast from Massachusetts to Florida.

Habitat. Tall grasses in salt marshes and tidal flats. Found among the *Spartina* grasses and rushes.

Size. $^3/_4$ to $^7/_8$ inch

Body Features. On the smaller end of the scale for this genus. Slender tegmina, bluntly rounded at the tip. The hind wings come to a slightly sharper point and usually extend past the tips. Males have the typical "humps" in the stridulary area; however, they are fairly weak.

Color. Green to *brown*. In green form, they are blue-green throughout with a yellow tinge on the end of the abdomen. The tegmina will have a yellow to brown wash in the upper area. There are often two thin, dark brown lateral stripes on the pronotal disc. In brown forms, the face, sides of head, sides of pronotum, legs, and hind femora are a pale tan. The top of the head and pronotal disc is dark brown, the latter with two thin brown lateral stripes, the outer edges bordered in white. The tegmina range from gray-brown to yellow-brown. There can be a wash of green beyond the male's stridulary area. The legs are often heavily speckled with dark dots. The antennae are pale to dark brown.

Male Cerci. The cerci are yellow to orange. The tip is strongly pinched and conical. The long inner surface of the area between the tip and tooth has a barely discernible bump. The tooth projects inward from about four-fifths the distance from the tip. The tooth is long with nearly parallel edges for most of its length and hooks strongly at the tip.

Ovipositor. Long, weakly curved, and usually extends beyond the wing tips, but sometimes falls short of them (relation between tip and wing tips variable, and not a reliable indicator of species); greenish brown in green females, and pale brown in brown females.

Call. Short, fluttery, buzzy sequences.

Similar Species. This species is confined to *salt marshes and tidal flats*. In green forms, it is best to look at its uniquely shaped male cerci.

Notes. Seaside Meadow Katydids feed exclusively on Smooth Cordgrass (*Spartina alterniflora*). A recent study suggests that their droppings fertilize the grass, creating a mutually beneficial cycle.

They are often found with their little cousins, the Saltmarsh Meadow Katydids.

Illustration on page 31.

Coneheads

Subfamily Copiphorinae

*T*he Copiphorinae of the Northeast comprise two genera:

Neoconocephalus—Coneheads or Conehead Katydids
Bucrates—Cattail Coneheads

Coneheads—Genus *Neoconocephalus*

Meaning "near or new *Conocephalus*," the *Neoconocephalus* were once considered *Conocephalus*, but were given their own genus based upon the shape of their cone. When you compare their cones with those of the Conocephalinae, it's obvious that most stand out in this regard. While not all of the cones are prominent, they all have a notch at the base. That notch is located just below the front surface, or face, of the cone.

The coneheads are found in a wide variety of wet and dry meadows, salt marshes, weedy fields and roadsides. One species, the Broad-tipped Conehead, calls from trees. These are large insects, ranging in length from one and a half to two and seven-eighths inches. Most begin calling at dusk and continue well into the night. Their food consists primarily of grass seeds. Seeing one eat the seeds off a grasshead reminds me of watching someone eating corn on the cob. They also eat the blades of grass, sedge seeds, and some flower heads.

Most species within this genus are fairly stout of body, long legged, and have hind wings slightly longer than the tegmina. All have wings that extend well beyond the tip of the abdomen. The tegmina and hind wings are long and come to a broad point. They resemble the tip of a blade of grass or sedge, which aids them in hiding from predators. While some coneheads will jump or fly to get away, most scuttle down the plant stem and stick their head, ostrichlike, into the base. The tegmina sticking up from the base of the tangled maze of stems and leaves become nearly unrecognizable as insect wings.

The coneheads are dimorphic, either green or brown. The green forms have painted faces of various shades of red and yellow. Other than that, the only noticeable pattern falls on the face of the cone. This pattern, or lack thereof, along with the shape of the cone, is the key to identifying the individual species.

The females lay their eggs between the stems and sheaths of the grasses, or in other plant matter close to the roots. Their ovipositors are long, straight, and sword-like, resembling oversize versions of the plastic cocktail swords used for spearing fruit in a mixed drink.

Conehead calls range from a gentle shushing to an earsplittingly loud buzz.

Identifying Coneheads

A key to separating the *Neoconocephalus* species is in the difference in the shape, size, and pattern in the cone, as illustrated to the left of the full profiles of the male and female. Note too the length and shape of the female's ovipositor, but bear in mind the position of the tip in relation to the wing tips can vary. We chose to illustrate the most typical forms we've encountered in the field and in museum specimens. In some species, the slight shape differences in the sides of the pronotum can also offer a clue.

Range. Rhode Island and south to Florida.

Habitat. Low in the herbaceous vegetation in fields, roadsides, and meadows.

Size. 1^1/$_2$ to 2 inches

Cone. Small, rounded, and only *slightly longer than wide.* The outer edge is rimmed with yellow or pale brown. A black or dark gray shallow crescent fills the upper tip of the cone.

Color. Grass green or pale brown, often with dark spots on the tegmina. A pale yellowish line runs from behind the eyes and along the dorsolateral edges of the pronotum. The lower area of the face may be orange and pink.

Ovipositor. Typically extends far beyond the tips of the wings and is infused with gray from about halfway from the base to the tip. It is equal in width throughout before reaching the tip.

Call. A steady, high-pitched, "live wire" buzz. Calls from late afternoon into the night.

Similar Species

Broad-tipped Conehead. While this species also has a very short, rounded cone, that cone is slightly broader than long. Broad-tipped Coneheads are also larger, 1^3/$_4$ to 2^5/$_8$ inches, and the ovipositor typically does not extend past the wing tips.

Marsh Conehead. While the Marsh Conehead is similar in size, the cone is more pinched and is without a black marking on the face. Its ovipositor typically falls short of the wing tips.

Notes. This is probably the most common conehead species within its range. They require little more than a patch of weeds on the side of the road. In some areas, if you roll down your car windows on a summer night, the call seems continuous and uninterrupted as you drive past one singing "round-tip" after another.

Illustration on page 37.

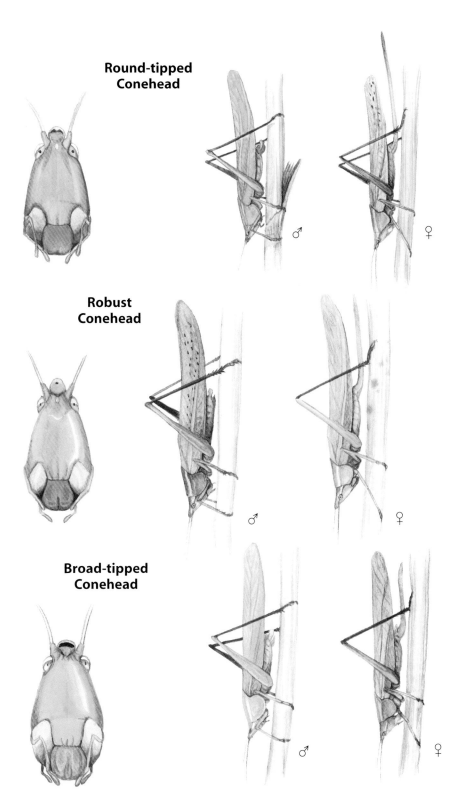

Round-tipped Conehead

♂   ♀

Robust Conehead

♂   ♀

Broad-tipped Conehead

♂   ♀

Range. Massachusetts and south to Florida.

Habitat. Fields, sandy river edges, salt marshes, wet meadows, and weedy roadsides.

Size. $2^1/_8$ to $2^7/_8$ inches

Cone. Tapers to a narrowly rounded tip, the outer edges paler than the face of the cone. The face is either *unmarked* or has a *small amount of black* at the very tip.

Color. Pale green to pale brown. Brown forms are often sprinkled with black dots. A pale line runs from behind the eyes and along the dorsolateral edges of the pronotum. Lower portion of face is often pale yellow to orange and raspberry red.

Ovipositor. Long, slender, either straight or turning gently upward. It is about equal in width throughout and typically falls short of the wing tips.

Call. A very loud, continuous buzz; about as pleasing a sound to the ear as that of a dentist's drill. In 1874, the entomologist Samuel Scudder compared it to the song of the Dog-day Cicada. The call begins in late afternoon and goes into the night.

Similar Species

> *Marsh Conehead.* See account on page 48.
>
> *Caudell's Conehead.* See account on page 40.

Notes. The first (and last) time I brought Robust Coneheads home, they resided in my studio. I had a male and a female set up in a plastic terrarium. The male wasted no time in calling. At first I was thrilled to be able to observe a calling male so closely. After about ten minutes I had enough—my ears were ringing. By day two, my family forced me to keep my studio door shut. By day three, I brought it over to Mike DiGiorgio's so he could paint it for this book. By day four, his wife left him. (Okay, not true.)

Illustration on page 37.

Range. New Jersey and south to Florida.

Habitat. High and low in trees; fields, edges of marshes, and forest undergrowth.

Size. $1^3/_4$ to $2^5/_8$ inches

Cone. *Slightly shorter than wide,* with a pale yellow or pale brown outer ridge. A heavy black arc is located near the top of the cone's face. This is the only conehead bearing a cone that is shorter than wide.

Color. Grass green to pale to gray-brown or yellow to reddish brown. Males often have a straight, dark line along the edge of the stridulary field just behind the pronotum. The lower area of the face can be yellow, orange, and raspberry red.

Ovipositor. Falls quite short of the wing tips and curves slightly up about two-thirds of the way before curving back down toward the tip.

Call. A steady buzz that seems to "trip" over itself. The stridulation is broken at regular intervals of one to two seconds. This is the only conehead with a call broken in this way.

Similar Species

> *Round-tipped Conehead.* See account on page 36.

Notes. It was early evening, and I was driving past a campground in Ocean County, New Jersey, when I heard a buzzing in a tree. I pulled the car over and got out to see if I could find out what it was. It was similar to a cicada, but they were done calling for the day. And the call was different; a buzz with brief rests in between. I was sure it was a conehead, but at the time I didn't know they called from trees! A conehead calling from the treetops seemed as unlikely to me as a true katydid calling from a grass stem. Unfortunately, there was no way to capture it that far up in the tree.

It was no doubt *triops*, and I've since found them in all kinds of trees, as well as where any respectable conehead belongs—in the grass.

Illustration on page 37.

Range. New Jersey and south to Florida.

Habitat. Marshes, bogs, wet meadows, and grassy fields.

Size. $2^1/_8$ to $2^3/_4$ inches

Cone. Tapers to a *blunt tip* and rimmed with yellow or pale brown. Face of cone is edged in black along the sides and tip.

Color. Rich green or varying shades of brown often with black mottling. The lower portion of the face is yellow and rose red.

Ovipositor. Long, fairly slender, often curving very gently up and then down toward the point. It approaches the wing tips, sometimes slightly surpassing them.

Call. A loud, slow, steady, and buzzy "dzeeet . . . dzeeet . . . dzeeet. . . ." The Long-beaked or Slightly Musical Conehead has a similar steady call, but there is a more lisping quality to it.

Similar Species

Eastern Swordbearer. See account on page 42.

Robust Conehead. While similar in size, they can be separated by the cone, which in the Robust comes to a sharper point and has little to no black on its face. The ovipositor typically falls short of the wing tips.

Notes. This conehead was named for Andrew Nelson Caudell (1872–1936). He was a lepidopterist and orthopterist most noted for his highly methodical nature. His data collections on the Orthoptera encompassed every minor detail of every species in the U.S. National Museum, where he was curator. It would rival the databases of today's computers. This spilled over into his nonprofessional life and it is said that his personal journals offered details on what happened in his life every single day for nearly forty years.

Illustration on page 41.

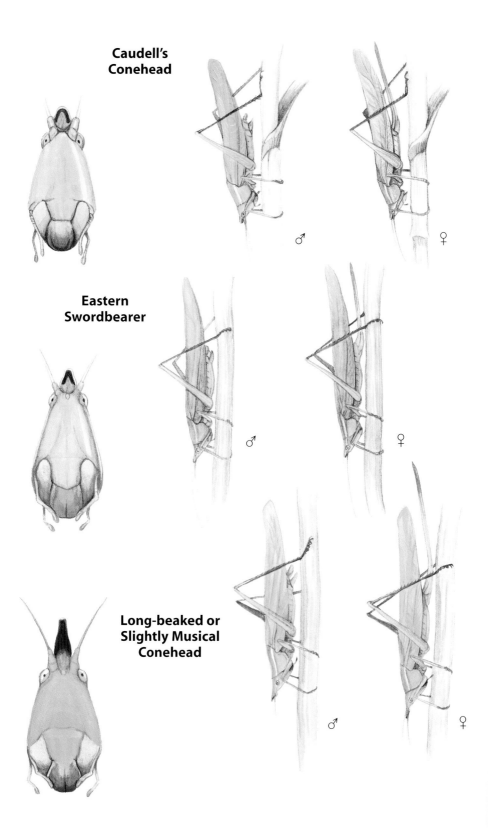

Caudell's Conehead

Eastern Swordbearer

Long-beaked or Slightly Musical Conehead

♂ ♀

♂ ♀

♂ ♀

Range. Canada and south to North Carolina.

Habitat. Fields, damp and drier meadows, and weedy roadsides.

Size. 1³/₄ to 2¹/₂ inches

Cone. Fairly long, pinched slightly about a third of the way from the top. The edges are rimmed in pale yellow. *Upper half* of the cone's face is edged in black, forming an inverted V.

Color. Grassy yellow-green with a yellowish stripe running from behind the eyes and along the dorsolateral edges of the pronotum. Many individuals are tan or pale brown, speckled with varying amounts of black dots on the tegmina. The lower area of face may be pale orange and rose pink.

Ovipositor. Long, slender, straight, and of even width throughout to the tip. It typically just barely passes the wing tips.

Call. A series of rapid, lisping buzzes, like a fast-moving train. Calls begin at dusk and go well into the night.

Similar Species

Marsh Conehead. See account on page 48.

Caudell's Conehead. While the pattern in the cone's face is similar, the cone is less pinched toward the top and more broadly rounded. Caudell's Conehead is also longer at 2¹/₈ to 2³/₄ inches, and if the conehead is north of New Jersey, it's not likely to be this species.

Slender Conehead. Similar in general shape, but the face of the cone is nearly or completely filled with black. Ovipositor is heavier and gently decurved about two-thirds the distance from the base.

Nebraska Conehead. Cone is similar in shape and pattern, but the heavy black inverted V extends down past the halfway point, nearly to the base.

Black-nosed Conehead. Cone is broader; the black in the cone is not restricted to the upper edges. Ovipositor is short and relatively wide. Black-nosed Coneheads are only found in tidal flats.

Notes. While I made the claim that the Round-tipped Conehead is probably our most common species within its range, the Eastern Swordbearer is the most common in the entire Northeast. Perhaps if the round-tips occurred north of Rhode Island, they would vie for that distinction, but they don't. Or at least I'm not aware of anyone finding one there yet.

Come late July or early August, the swordbearers seem to just drop from the sky. One evening they are not there, and then they arrive and seem to be everywhere. Naturally, they were there the whole time as nymphs, but it appears they have a well-synchronized final molt.

The swordbearers also seem to get along well with others, as their calls can often be heard mingling with those of a number of different species.

Illustration on page 41.

Long-beaked or Slightly Musical Conehead
Neoconocephalus exiliscanorus

Range. Connecticut and south to Texas.

Habitat. Marshes, wetland thickets, and fields.

Size. $1^7/8$ to $2^7/8$ inches

Cone. *Very long and tapering.* Sometimes the sides are pinched. Face of the cone is either completely black or four-fifths black from the tip down, the lower border of that black forming a shallow inverted V. The Long-beaked or Slightly Musical Conehead has the longest cone of all the species.

Color. Raw pea green with a pale line running along the dorsolateral edges of the pronotum. Some individuals or populations are cocoa brown with black spots on the wings. Lower portion of face can be pale to deep yellow and deep red raspberry.

Ovipositor. Long, straight, and slender with a touch of reddish brown at the tip. It extends very far past the wing tips.

Call. A steady series of lispy "ziits," fairly rapid on warm evenings. Calls begin at dusk and go well into the evening. See the accounts of the Nebraska Conehead (page 46) and the Caudell's Conehead (page 40) for descriptions of their similar calls.

Similar Species

   Slender Conehead. See account on page 44.

   Nebraska Conehead. See account on page 46.

   Robust Conehead. The Robust Conehead is also large, but its cone is much shorter in comparison to that of a Long-beak's, and the face of the cone is not filled with black. The tip of the ovipositor generally falls short of the wing tips.

Notes. Although the alternate name for this conehead, "Slightly Musical Conehead," is a better translation of the scientific name, I still prefer "Long-beaked Conehead." In my mind, that long cone is what really makes this insect stand apart from the others. I also find the call very pleasing, and there are other species I would deem far less musical than this one. "Slightly Musical," however, is a step up from the more literal translation of its name, "Unmusical," which was what they were called prior to the descriptive upgrade.

Illustration on page 41.

Range. Vermont and south to Maryland.

Habitat. Fresh and saltwater grassy marshes and bogs.

Size. $1^3/_4$ to $2^5/_8$ inches

Cone. Long, slender, and tapering strongly to a rounded point. Face of cone is *almost entirely jet black.*

Color. Grass green or cocoa to yellow-brown. A yellowish stripe runs along the dorso-lateral edges of the pronotum. Lower area of face may be yellow and deep red.

Ovipositor. Somewhat heavy and slightly decurved about two-thirds the distance from the base. The tip lines up close to the wing tips.

Call. A loud, high-pitched, continuous buzz. Call begins in the late afternoon and continues into the night.

Similar Species

Eastern Swordbearer. See account on page 42.

Nebraska Conehead. Cone is very similar—long and tapered, with the face of the cone mostly black. A good way to distinguish the Nebraska Conehead from the Slender Conehead is by comparing the sides of the pronotum. In Nebraska, the lower lobe toward the rear has a slight convex bump that points down toward the base of the hind femur. The notch above that lobe (humeral sinus) is shallow and not sharply angled. In the Slender Conehead, the lower lobe of the pronotum is *evenly rounded* and the notch almost forms a *sharp right angle.*

If you have a female Nebraska Conehead, note that the ovipositor extends considerably past the wing tips.

If the conehead is in upland, drier habitat, you can most likely rule out the Slender Conehead, which is restricted to wetland areas.

Lastly, the call of the Nebraska Conehead is broken into short buzzes, unlike the continuous buzz of the Slender Conehead.

Long-beaked Conehead. Cone is also long and tapered, with the face of the cone mostly black. The cone in this species, however, is considerably longer and comes to a sharper point. The ovipositor extends very far beyond the wing tips.

Notes. *Lyristes* was once considered to be a subspecies of *nebrascensis*, based upon their similar appearance. A closer look found a number of differences between the two (as shown in this book), including song and habitat, so it was elevated to full species.

Illustration on page 45.

Slender
Conehead

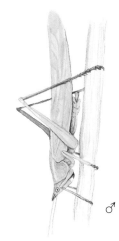

♂

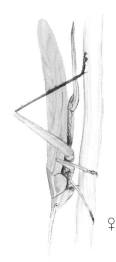

♀

Nebraska
Conehead

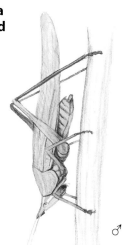

♂

♀

Black-nosed
Conehead

♂

♀

Range. Pennsylvania and south to western Virginia. Absent from the coast.

Habitat. High and low in weedy fields and roadsides; edges of freshwater marshes.

Size. $1^3/_4$ to $2^1/_4$ inches

Cone. Long, pinched for about four-fifths its length, coming to a broadly rounded top. The face of the cone is *nearly all black,* often forming a thick inverted V, or sometimes forming a "widow's peak."

Color. Bright green or pale or yellowish brown. A pale narrow line runs from behind the eyes and along the dorsolateral edges of the pronotum. Lower section of face is often yellow-orange and deep red.

Ovipositor. Long and slender, fairly evenly wide throughout and curving slightly upward. It extends beyond the wing tips.

Call. A steady series of high, loud buzzes, each with a second or two pause in between. There's a somewhat angry quality to it, although that would be an unfair characterization to place on an innocent bug. The Slightly Musical Conehead has a similar, steady call, but with a more lisping quality. Caudell's Conehead is also broken into sections, but each "dzeeet" is considerably shorter in duration, and given in more rapid sequence.

Similar Species

Slender Conehead. See account on page 44.

Eastern Swordbearer. See account on page 42.

Black-nosed Conehead. Cone is wider in relation to its length and tapers less toward the tip. The ovipositor is short, straight, and wide.

Long-beaked Conehead. While both species have a long, black cone, the cone of the Long-beaked Conehead is considerably longer and appears less broad at the tip. Its ovipositor greatly exceeds the wing tips.

Notes. This species finds itself far from the Atlantic coast and at the western end of its range for this book. I don't know why they haven't ventured farther east. The habitat and climate they find in their current range is easily duplicated along the coast, and there are no mountain ranges or other apparent obstacles in their way.

I first became acquainted with Nebraska Coneheads along the Skyline Drive in the Shenandoah Mountains in Virginia. They began calling at dusk from the grassy edges of the road and were found side by side with calling Round-tipped Coneheads, the latter's call being nearly drowned out by their neighbors.

Illustration on page 45.

Black-nosed Conehead   *Neoconocephalus melanorhinus*

Range. Hugs the coast from New Jersey to Florida.

Habitat. Among the grasses and sedges in tidal flats.

Size. $1^5/_8$ to $2^1/_2$ inches

Cone. About twice as long as its width at the base, tapering gently toward a broadly rounded tip. The face of the cone is usually at least two-thirds black, often forming a very shallow inverted V. Sometimes the black fills the entire face of the cone. This is frequently the case in brown individuals. In some individuals, that V forming the lower border of black is not inverted but instead forms a widow's peak.

Color. Varying shades of brown or grass green. A pale yellow line runs along the dorsolateral edges of the pronotum. Males often have a straight, dark line along the edge of the stridulary field just behind the pronotum. Lower area of face may be yellow and deep red.

Ovipositor. Rather short, straight, and wide. It does not extend past the wing tips.

Call. A continuous, high-pitched electric buzz. It is similar to that of the Round-tipped Conehead; however, unlike the Black-nosed Conehead, the Round-tipped Conehead is not restricted to tidal flats.

Similar Species

> *Eastern Swordbearer.* See account on page 42.
>
> *Slender Conehead.* See account on page 44.
>
> *Nebraska Conehead.* See account on page 46.

Notes. Sadly, the best places for finding Black-nosed Coneheads are closed to the public just when they're getting going. New Jersey has a number of wildlife refuges along the shore where one can find the perfect habitat for this species without leaving the car. The Cape May and Brigantine National Wildlife Refuges allow one to drive slowly along the edges of salt marshes, windows down, no cars pushing you to go faster—but they close at dusk. It's a shame that access to some of the best habitat in this country is unavailable to us at night without acquiring special permission (which I usually end up doing).

If you want to find Black-nosed Coneheads, your best bet is to search just outside the parks and look for pull-offs along roads that hug the salt marshes. Be prepared to see the flashing lights of police cars, though. What you're doing looks very suspicious. I've always found our law enforcement officers to be understanding of what I'm up to, however, if not somewhat amused.

Illustration on page 45.

Range. New Jersey and south to Florida.

Habitat. Bogs, marshes, and other grassy wet areas.

Size. $1^1/_2$ to $2^3/_4$ inches

Cone. Short, stout, with the upper third slightly pinched, tapering to a bluntly rounded tip. The outer edge is rimmed with yellow and the face of the cone contains *no black.*

Color. Females are usually grass green, while the males tend to be pale to dark brown. A yellow line runs from behind the eyes and along the dorsolateral edges of the pronotum. Lower area of face may be red, orange, and/or purple.

Ovipositor. Short, broad, growing wider at about two-thirds the distance from the base before coming to a point. The shape brings to mind a *broadsword.* The tip of the ovipositor typically falls short of the wing tips. About a third of the length toward the tip is rusty in color.

Call. A sustained, somewhat weak, high-pitched "zeeeeeeeeeeee. . . ." Higher pitched than the similar sounding Round-tipped Conehead.

Similar Species

Round-tipped Conehead. See comparison in account on page 36.

Eastern Swordbearer. While the shape and size are similar between these two species, the Eastern Swordbearer has an arched band of black in the cone. The ovipositor is long, slender, and of the same width throughout its length.

Robust Conehead. Both have clean, pointed cones, but the Robust Conehead is larger with a more slender ovipositor that is equal in width throughout its length. They can also be told apart by the sides of their pronotum. In the Marsh Conehead, the area between the lowest point (somewhat toward the rear of the lobe) and where it turns in to form an indentation (humeral sinus) is bluntly rounded. In the Robust Conehead, that same area forms an evenly rounded arc.

Notes. This species can be a challenge to catch at night. They are very aware of your approach, and upon spotting you, they stop calling and take evasive action. I was being repeatedly bested by one calling male along a pond in Maryland. Finally giving up on sneaking up on him, I started swinging my net in the tall grasses. This is always a last resort—an act of desperation. If you miss, you send everything down into the roots, where they stay until they feel it's safe to emerge. I checked my net and saw that I had managed to catch a female, but I was hoping to catch a male so I could record it in my studio. Knowing I had ruined any chance at getting the singer, I went back to my car. As I drove away, I heard him calling back at the edge of the lake. He won that one.

Illustration on page 49.

**Marsh
Conehead**

♂

♀

**Cattail
Conehead**

♂

♀

(short-winged form)

Cattail Coneheads—Genus *Bucrates*

The *Bucrates* are primarily a South American genus, with one representative ranging as far north as New Jersey. Cattail coneheads and their kin are separated from the *Neoconocephalus* coneheads by the lack of a notch at the base of the cone.

Cattail Conehead　　　　　　　　　　　　　　　　*Bucrates malivolans*

Range. New Jersey and south to Florida.

Habitat. Marshes and wetland edges, among the palmettos and saw grass farther south.

Size. Short-winged form: $1^1/_8$ to $1^3/_4$ inches
　　　Long-winged form: $1^3/_4$ to $2^3/_4$ inches

Cone. Short and bluntly rounded. It *lacks a prominent gap* between the base of the cone and the top of the head. There is no black on the front surface.

Color. Pale yellow-brown to deep brown. A darker stripe runs along the dorsolateral edges of the pronotum. Some individuals and populations are green.

Description. There are two forms of this conehead; the long-winged and short-winged. In the short-winged form, the wing tips reach only about as far as the abdomen. In the less common long-winged form, the wing tips extend about one-third of their length beyond the abdomen.

　　　The ovipositor is long, broad, and extends past the wing tips, as to be expected in the short-winged form, and still considerably in the long-winged form.

Call. A steady, questioning, "tchir-tchir-tchir . . . ?"

Similar Species. This is the only representative of the genus *Bucrates* in the Northeast.

Notes. On the surface, one may look at these Cattail Coneheads as a variant on the *Neoconocephalus* theme, based upon their shared large size. The *Neoconocephalus*, however, do not have a long-winged *and* short-winged form. Yes, there are variations in their wing length, but not to the point where they are considered different morphs. *Malivolans* actually seem to have more in common with their diminutive cousins, the *Conocephalus* (smaller meadow katydids). Many of the latter also have two wing morphs, and all lack the gap on the face of the cone. While the taxonomists may want to throttle me for saying this, I think of the Cattail Coneheads as "big smaller meadow katydids."

Illustration on page 49.

False Katydids
Subfamily Phaneropterinae

I always try to pay attention to the names given to insects. Not just the common names, but the scientific names, as they often share a certain aspect of that group that helps set it apart from others. Phaneropterinae, which contains three genera described in this book, means "visible wing." At first, you may wonder what the big deal is about knowing you can see the wings. When can't you? (Okay, sometimes you can't.) What nineteenth-century entomologist J. G. Audinet-Serville was referring to when he named this subfamily, however, were the hind wings, which extend past the tegmina. So this subfamily is named for the little section of hind wing that is visible as a result of its being longer than the tegmina. Fortunately, when it comes to identifying the species, there is more to go on than that.

Round-headed Katydids—Genus *Amblycorypha*

Those in this genus, named for the rounded "forehead," or *fastidium*, are about medium to large in size when compared with other katydids. The *Amblycorypha* are fairly robust, and have broad, elliptical leaflike wings. They tend to live in the lower vegetation—meadows, weedy fields, edges of woodlands—but can also be heard at various levels in deciduous trees. They eat a wide variety of leaves and flowers, and when given the opportunity, will feed on fruit with great zeal.

The movements of round-headed katydids are slow and deliberate. It appears as if they are sneaking about. For example, when going from one leaf to another, an individual will extend a foreleg, slowly rocking back and forth like a leaf in the breeze, until it alights on the surface. Then the next leg follows in the same manner, and so on until they're where they need to be. They can fly, but are rarely seen doing so.

The tegmina form a variety of oval shapes, and are always widest in the middle and broadly rounded at the tips. The hind wings extend past the tegmina and come to more of a point. While typically green, there are many instances where the entire insect will be yellow, brown, and even pink. The stridulary area on the male tegmina is brown, and is traversed by a heavy, green vein; female tegmina are uniformly green (unless it is a yellow, brown, or pink morph).

The female's ovipositor is sickle shaped, broad, and curves upward. The tip comes to a broad point and is armed with short teeth above and below. Eggs are deposited in the damp soil at the base of plants.

The calls of *Amblycorypha* are easy to hear, and sometimes hard to ignore. They range from sputtering rattles to harsh, wet ticks.

This genus can be confused with the *Scudderia*, or bush katydids (see identification clues in that section), and the *Microcentrum*, or angle-wings. To tell them apart from the latter, see the table below.

Amblycorypha	*Microcentrum*
Wings are oblong; any bumps on the upper or lower edges are rounded.	Wings are oblong, but noticeably angled, somewhat diamond or spearhead shaped.
When lined up with the center of the tegmina, the tip of the hind femur makes it to the rear quarter.	When lined up with the center of the tegmina, the tip of the hind femur falls short of the rear quarter.
The upper (dorsal) edge of the front and middle tibiae will either be flat, or will have a slight groove.	The upper edge of the front and middle tibiae will be rounded.
The distance between the lowest segments of the antennae will be two times or *less* than the width of the lowest (base) antenna segment.	The distance between the lowest segments of the antennae will be two times or *more* than the width of the lowest (base) antenna segment.
Ovipositor is long, gently curved, comes to a point, and has teeth on the upper and lower edges of the tip.	Ovipositor is short, bends sharply upward, is blunt, with teeth only at the terminal edge.

Range. Canada and south to Florida.

Habitat. Edges of salt- and freshwater marshes, wet and dry meadows, shrubby fields, edges of woodlands.

Size. $1^5/_8$ to 2 inches

Description. Pale leaf green (rarely bright pink or yellow). The dorsolateral ridges of the pronotal disc are usually *rounded,* sometimes bordered with a dark line. In individuals with more keeled ridges, they tend to grow rounder toward the front or rear of the pronotum. The stridulary field in males is dark brown with a green crossvein. That stridulary field tends to be considerably larger in area when compared with the area of the pronotal disc. Six to twelve heavy teeth line the lower ridge of the hind femur. The tips of the femora rarely reach the tips of the tegmina.

    The wings are widely oval and between *three and four times longer than wide.*

    The ovipositor is long, curved upward, and comes to a slightly rounded point. The teeth, found only toward the tip, are relatively short, fairly heavy, and somewhat irregularly spaced.

Call. A short, harsh "ski-di-deet!" or "skritch-it" given at irregular intervals. Sings mostly at night.

Similar Species

    Carinate Katydid. It is nearly identical in appearance to the Oblong-winged Katydid. It is best separated by the sharply angled (carinate) ridges of the dorsolateral edges of the pronotum. In Oblong-wings, those ridges are more rounded. The male stridulary area is not much greater in area than the pronotal disc. The ovipositor is usually slightly less pointed, the teeth are heavier and spaced somewhat more irregularly and farther apart.

    In the Northeast, Carinate Katydids usually occur later in the season than Oblong-wings.

    Round-winged Katydids. Tegmina are less oblong, less than three times long as wide. The tip of the hind femur, when lined up with the center of the tegmina, either reaches or extends past tegmina tips; not so with the Oblong-winged Katydid. Four to five small teeth line the lower ridge of the hind femur. The ovipositor is slightly more gently curved, slightly more rounded at the tip, and deeply serrated.

    Angle-wings. The two species in our area share the rounded heads and long, broad tegmina with the Oblong-winged Katydids. As their name suggests, however, the wings are more angular. See more detailed differences between angle-wings and round-headed katydids on pages 51 and 52.

Notes. [Author's note: Since this is the illustrator's favorite species, I let him take this one.] Of all of the night-singing insects that I have studied, painted, and observed, the Oblong-winged Katydid is probably my favorite. As a child, I can remember its "skiii-dikk" call floating into my bedroom window on muggy summer evenings. For years I wondered about the shadowy creature that was the author of this wonderful call. I finally hunted down a large camouflaged katydid perched on top of our lilac bush. I captured the striking insect and decided that it would make a great pet. I became fascinated with its catlike movements as it preened and climbed up the side of the cage. In some ways, it reminded me of a ballet dancer.

My family's complaints about its relentless nighttime calling finally forced me to release it back into the wild. Even today, on a warm August evenings, "skiii-dikk" brings back fond childhood memories and makes me feel that all is well with the world.

Illustration on page 55.

Carinate Katydid   *Amblycorypha carinata*

Range. Massachusetts and south to Florida.

Habitat. Edges of salt- and freshwater marshes, wet and dry meadows, shrubby fields, edges of woodlands.

Size. $1^5/_8$ to $1^7/_8$ inches

Description. Pale leaf green (rarely bright pink or yellow), a heavy brown, sometimes a dark, two-toned or single stripe runs along the dorsolateral edges of the pronotal disc. Those lateral ridges are very prominent (carinate), and *keeled along most of their entire length.* The stridulary field in males is dark brown with a green crossvein. That stridulary area is about the same size as the pronotal disc. Six to twelve heavy teeth line the lower ridge of the hind femur.

The wings are widely oval and between three and four times longer than wide.

The ovipositor is long, curved upward, and comes to a point. The teeth, found only toward the tip, are relatively short, fine, and evenly spaced close together.

Call. A high, somewhat harsh, lisping "zit," or "zi-deet," usually repeated steadily with a few seconds in between.

Similar Species

Oblong-winged Katydid. See account on page 53.

Notes. I knew from specimen records that members of this species should be in my area. What I did not know was how prevalent they are! This became apparent when I came home one night in mid-October and found one at the front door porch light. This inspired me to check what I'd dismissed as late-season Oblong-wings in my yard. It turns out they were all Carinate Katydids.

There's just a smattering of papers on this species, most of them dating back to when *Amblycorypha floridana carinata* was considered a subspecies of *Amblycorypha oblongifolia.* Its members have since been elevated to a full species.

There are two attributes of this species I've noted missing in the literature. One of them is their "shyness." *Oblongifolia* katydids will call amid minor disturbances from the likes of us bipeds. *Carinata* do not, in the field or in captivity. It seems as if they see you way before you wish to be seen. The other thing I've noted is the lateness of calling in the Northeast. The entomological journal *Psyche* mentions that they are active in November in Nantucket, Massachusetts.

Illustration on page 55.

Carinate Katydid

Oblong-winged Katydid

Rattler Round-winged Katydid

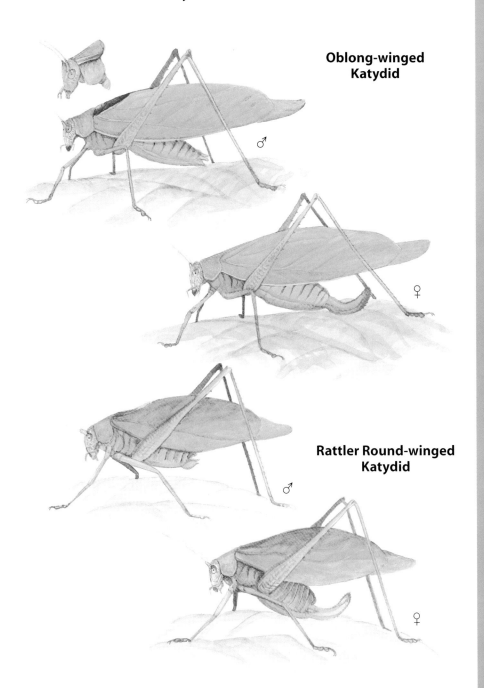

Rattler Round-winged Katydid   *Amblycorypha rotundifolia*

Range. Maine and south to western Georgia.

Habitat. Upland meadows, dry, shrubby fields, and edges of deciduous forests.

Size. $1^{1}/_{4}$ to $1^{1}/_{2}$ inches

Description. Pale leaf green (rarely bright pink or yellow), body a little paler than tegmina. The tegmina are oval and *less than three times longer than wide.* The tip of the hind femur, when lined up with the center of the tegmina, extends past the tegmina tips. The male stridulary area is brown with a green crossvein. Four to five small teeth line the lower ridge of the hind femur. The ovipositor curves gently upward and forms a blunt point at the tip, which is deeply serrated.

Call. A high, sputtering rattle. It often gives a few introductory sputters, like someone trying to start a tiny flooded two-cycle engine. Then it gives a more sustained sputter, lasting several seconds. Sings at night.

There is another nearly identical species called the **Clicker Round-winged Katydid (*Amblycorypha alexanderi*)** found from southern Pennsylvania and south to Florida. It is best separated from the Rattler Round-headed Katydid by its call, a steady series of high "zits."

Similar Species

Oblong-winged and Carinate Katydids. See accounts on pages 53 and 54.

Notes. The Rattler Round-wings remind me of cats. They move slowly and deliberately, seem little concerned with what's going on around them, and are very fastidious, spending a lot of time grooming their legs and long antennae. I always look for one when leading a nature walk, as it will typically allow me to urge it onto my hand and pass it from person to person. I'm very fond of these katydids, and enjoy repaying them for their "good nature" with a treat of sliced apple.

Illustration on page 55.

Angle-wings or Angle-winged Katydids—Genus *Microcentrum*

Microcentrum means "small point," referring to the distinctively pointed wing tips. These are very attractive insects, outdoing, in my opinion, the leaves they've evolved to mimic. Unfortunately, we rarely get to see them, as they are arboreal in nature and rarely descend from the treetops. In areas where those treetops are relatively low, however, such as fruit orchards, they are more easily found.

The Angle-wings, or Angle-winged Katydids, tend to be on the larger end of the katydid scale, and while their bodies are very robust, that trait is hidden by those "slimming" angular tegmina. The tegmina are diamond or spearhead shaped and taper to a broad point in the rear. That point is usually "sharpened" by the tips of the protruding hind wings.

These insects feed on the leaves of deciduous plants, as well as fruit and flowers. The female deposits her flat, oval, overlapping eggs in rows on leaves and stems.

Their calls usually involve some form of ticking or rattling.

The *Microcentrum* share the same subfamily, Phaneropterinae, with two other genera: *Scudderia*, the bush katydids, and *Amblycorypha*, the round-headed katydids. Characteristics used to separate them are covered in detail within the accounts of those groups.

Identifying Angle-wings

While there are a number of ways to tell the difference between the Greater and Lesser Angle-wing Katydids, a simple and reliable technique is to look at the pronotal disc. This is the dorsal face of the pronotum, which is different in shape in the two species. The disc is represented next to the illustrations of the male and female.

Range. Southern New York and south to Florida.

Habitat. Middle height to the crowns of deciduous trees.

Size. $1^7/8$ to 2 inches

Body Features. The tegmina are shaped like a thin spearhead, rounded at the tip. The hind wings extend beyond the outer leaflike wings adding a point to the "spearhead." The front edge of the pronotal disc forms a single, concave arc, with *no tooth*. The body is very robust.

Color. Tegmina and tips of hind wings are pale green. The head and body are often lighter in color. A pale stripe begins behind the eyes and extends along the dorsolateral ridges of the pronotum. The stridulary area in the male is *dark brown*. Sometimes there is pink along the upper edges of the femora. The tip of the ovipositor is raspberry red.

Ovipositor. Short and bends sharply upward. The tip comes to a bluntly rounded point with fine teeth only toward the end.

Call. A rapid, lispy rattle, like a rushed version of the Common True Katydid's call, which is often heard in the background while this species is calling. Calls mostly at night.

Similar Species

Greater Angle-wing. This species extends farther north, is larger, and the male stridulary area is green, not brown. An angle-wing north of southern Pennsylvania and Long Island, New York, is likely to be a Greater Angle-wing. Its wings are wider in relation to their length. The pronotal disc shapes are distinctively different between the two species. In the Greater Angle-wing, the front of the disc forms a weak wave with a central "tooth" pointing toward the head. In the Lesser Angle-wing, the front of the disc forms a single, concave arc, and lacks the tooth.

The ovipositor in the Greater Angle-wing is also short and bends sharply upward. The tip is less rounded, however, appearing as if it was snipped off. You will notice, too, that the cerci in the male Greater Angle-wing wind in and then out. In the Lesser Angle-wing, they curve gently inward.

Oblong-winged Katydid. This species, and other *Amblycorypha*, share the rounded heads and broad wings with the angle-wing katydids. See more detailed differences between angle-wings and round-headed katydids in the section on the *Amblycorypha* genus on pages 51 and 52.

Notes. I was visiting my aunt in Lynbrook in Long Island, New York, and heard a Lesser Angle-wing calling from a dogwood tree on her front lawn. This was the farthest north I'd ever heard one, and I was eager to catch it. Catching a katydid up in a tree with my bare hands, however, was beyond my abilities. The thing about katydids, though, is they can be appreciated whether you see them or not. Once I reminded myself of that, I was able to enjoy the experience without risk of broken bones.

Illustration on page 59.

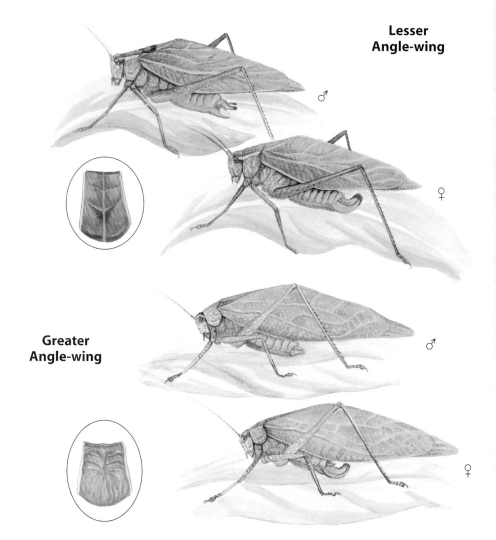

**Lesser
Angle-wing**

♂

♀

**Greater
Angle-wing**

♂

♀

Greater Angle-wing

Microcentrum rhombifolium

Range. Connecticut and south to Florida.

Habitat. Top of shrubs and the crowns of deciduous trees.

Size. 2 to $2^1/_2$ inches

Body Features. The tegmina are shaped like a round-tipped rhombus (hence the name *Rhombifolium*, meaning "rhombus-shaped leaf"). The hind wings extend beyond the tegmina and taper to a point. The front edge of the pronotal disc forms a weak wave with a *central "tooth"* pointing toward the head.

Color. Rich, deep green, with a pale stripe running from behind the eyes and along the dorsolateral edges of the pronotum. The male stridulary area is the *same color* as the rest of the wing. The tip of the ovipositor is raspberry red.

Ovipositor. Short and bends sharply upward. The tip is blunt, as if it was snipped off, with fine teeth only towards the end.

Call. This species has two calls. One is an uneven, rapid series of ticks, sounding like two pebbles being tapped together (or a Geiger counter, which we've nicknamed this species). The other call is a lisping "tzip," which may be repeated a number of times. Calls mostly at night.

Similar Species

Lesser Angle-wing. See account on page 58.

Notes. When Mike DiGiorgio and I set out on the eight-year journey to create this book, our very first stop was at a friend's front yard. Mike had his recorder with him and was trying to pick up the calls of a Greater Angle-wing in the trees. It was too far up, however, and calling too infrequently.

Over the years, the two of us, together and on our own, attempted to get recordings of Greater Angle-wings in the field. We got them, but there was always a plane going overhead, cars going by, dogs barking, and leaves rattling in the wind. And when these weren't a problem, there was the challenge of trying to pick up those little "ticks" from among the ever-present rasping of the True Katydids.

And then, one October night, we headed out one more time. Our deadline for this book loomed just months away, and it was time to finish our writing and painting. We found ourselves on a little footbridge in Madison, Connecticut. This was the last night before an oncoming cold spell that would silence everything for two weeks. A Greater Angle-wing called from about twenty feet directly across from us; loud, clear, and uninterrupted. It's the call you hear on the accompanying CD.

We had come full circle, ending on the note we'd begun.

Illustration on page 59.

Bush Katydids—Genus *Scudderia*

The bush katydid genus of *Scudderia* is an honorific title, meant as a tip of the hat to one of the more prolific contributors to Orthoptera research, and a fellow New Englander, Samuel Scudder. The common name of "bush katydid" refers to their habitat. These are medium-sized leaf mimics that inhabit lower vegetation. They can be found in goldenrod meadows, weedy pastures, and low branches at the edge of forests; mostly in places where you don't have to crane your neck up too far to see them. There are, of course, exceptions. The bush katydids feed on a wide variety of deciduous leaves; sassafras is a favorite, so too is cherry, but many of the leaves in and around woodlands are food. The Treetop Katydid is an exception, feeding on the needles of conifers.

What most *Scudderia* species have in common from a morphological standpoint are the following: long, nearly parallel tegmina; a long, upward-curved subgenital (lower tip of abdomen) plate that meets an extended, often-notched supra-anal plate (last segment, or tip, of upper abdomen); and a broad, laterally flattened ovipositor that bends upward.

And, once again, there are exceptions to those descriptions, but that's what keeps life interesting.

Bush katydids are not particularly loud singers, and the word "sing" is a stretch when describing their call. They are basically tickers and "shishers." But their call adds a bit of sparse rhythm to the insect concert.

The best way to tell one bush katydid from another, aside from its song, is by looking at the male supra-anal plate, which, fortunately for us, is easy to see. What you need to do is look at the tip of the abdomen from the top. Sometimes you can see it when the katydid is perched, but it is often necessary to hold the insect in a better position to view the supra-anal plate. This is the upper (supra) apparatus extending from the tip of the abdomen (anal—meaning toward the rear), which presents itself in a variety of double-pronged shapes. Each species has a distinctively shaped supra-anal plate, and by comparing it with the illustrations in this book, you will able to sort them out. The subgenital plate is the longer apparatus extending from the ventral tip of the abdomen. It curves upward, sometimes reaching the supra-anal plate.

The female ovipositors are curved and knife-thin. This design allows them to lay their flattened eggs in between the layers of leaves. Once, when keeping a pair of Fork-tailed Bush Katydids in a cage, I discovered that the female had oviposited her eggs in between the layers of paper towel at the bottom. While the ovipositors are somewhat uniquely shaped for each species, the females are best identified by their association with the males.

The bush katydids can most easily be confused with the other two genera in the "visible wing" subfamily. Those would be the *Amblycorypha* (round-headed katydids) and the *Microcentrum* (angle-wings). To separate them from those two genera, first look at the tegmina, which are the biggest standout features of a katydid:

Scudderia	Amblycorypha and Microcentrum
Tegmina are slender and the upper and lower edges are parallel or somewhat parallel.	Tegmina more broad, or oval, and distinctively broader in the middle.
There is very little space between the antenna bases. That space is always *less* than the width of the base (lowest) segment of the antenna.	The area between the antenna bases is always much *greater* than the width of the base segment of the antenna.
	To learn how to separate the *Amblycorypha* from the *Microcentrum*, refer back to the *Amblycorypha* account on pages 51 and 52.

Identifying Bush Katydids

Each species has a distinctively shaped supra-anal plate. Look at the dorsal surface of that appendage and compare it with the representation shown next to the illustrations of the male and female. It is often necessary to have the katydid in hand to see the supra-anal plate from this vantage point. Gently pinch together the tips of the knees (hind femora) between thumb and forefinger. It helps if you can also include a bit of the tegmina in your fingertips. See illustration on the opposite page.

Take note of the shape of the pronotal disc (upper surface of pronotum) and shape and angle of the ovipositor as well.

CURVE-TAILED BUSH KATYDID

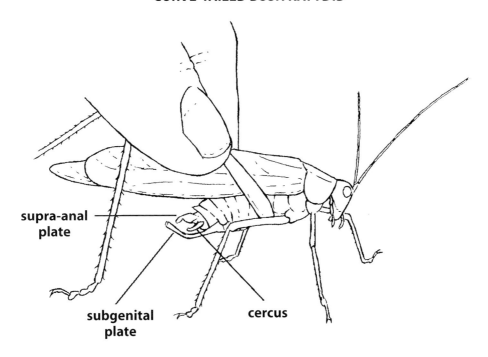

supra-anal plate

subgenital plate

cercus

DORSAL VIEW OF
SUPRA-ANAL PLATE

DORSAL VIEW

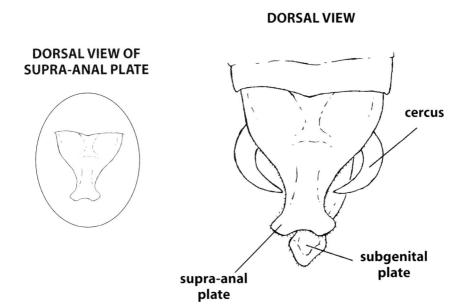

cercus

supra-anal plate

subgenital plate

Northern Bush Katydid   *Scudderia septentrionalis*

Range. Canada to South Carolina.

Habitat. Tall shrubs along woodland edges and various heights in the tree canopies of deciduous woods.

Size. $1^3/_8$ to $1^5/_8$ inches

Description. Rich green with thick veins. A deep yellow stripe runs along the dorsolateral edges of the pronotum. The tegmina are relatively short and broad, with a slight bulge along the bottom edge about halfway from the base.

Male Supra-anal Plate. The Northern Bush Katydid is the only bush katydid in this group *without an appendage projecting from this area.* The plate comes to a truncated, wavy end.

Ovipositor. Long, curving evenly and gently, tip pointing more to the rear horizon than up.

Pronotal Disc. Narrows slightly toward the head.

Call. A rather complex call for a bush katydid: a series of wet ticks followed by a rapid succession of "dzee-dzee-dzee-dzee. . . ." Calls from late afternoon into the night.

Similar Species. All other male bush katydids have an extended appendage from the supra-anal plate. All other female bush katydids have more sharply angled, upturned ovipositors.

Notes. This was often referred to as "rare" in much of the early literature on katydids. A season rarely passes, however, without my finding several of them. I suppose in some cases rarity is a relative term and subjective to one's travels. I often find them on the side of my house during the day, perhaps having been attracted to my porch light the previous night.

Illustration on page 65.

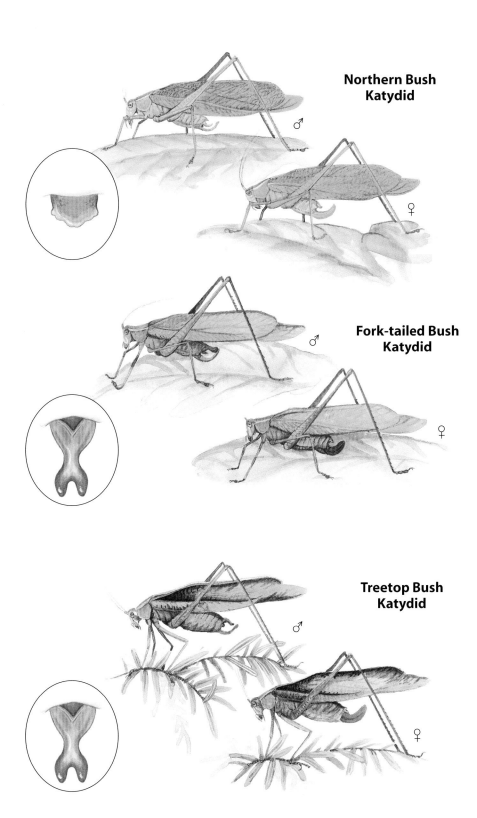

Northern Bush Katydid

♂

♀

Fork-tailed Bush Katydid

♂

♀

Treetop Bush Katydid

♂

♀

Fork-tailed Bush Katydid   *Scudderia furcata*

Range. Throughout the United States.

Habitat. Weedy fields, thickets, forest edges, and meadows.

Size. $1^3/8$ to 2 inches

Description. Rich, deep green, sometimes with pale yellow along the lateral edges of the pronotum. Wings are narrow and equally wide throughout their length and about four and a half times longer than wide. The hind femora are often brownish red.

Male Supra-anal Plate. Large, inflated, lobes form a *deep U* (or fork, as its name "fork-tailed" suggests), which surrounds the sides of the subgenital plate.

Ovipositor. Short, bent sharply (more than 90 degrees) upward a little past a quarter its length from the base. It becomes wider after the bend than at its base. Sometimes purple or raspberry red.

Pronotal Disc. Nearly parallel along the dorsolateral edges, tapering only slightly toward the head. It is a little longer than broad.

Call. A wet, isolated "tzip," sometimes given in a sequence, often irregular, with several seconds in between. Calls late in the day and into the night.

Similar Species

Curve-tailed Bush Katydid. Similar in size and shape, but tegmina are slightly less parallel along the top and bottom. They begin to taper more strongly about three-quarters from the base. The lobes in the male supra-anal plate form only a shallow V, are blunt, and turn away from each other. The ovipositor turns upward with a slightly less sharp angle and it's of a relatively equal width throughout its length. The pronotal disc is distinctively more long than broad and tapers more strongly toward the head.

Texas Bush Katydid. Tegmina are not as consistently parallel, the lower edge bows gently just past the halfway point. The tegmina are five to five and a half times longer than their greatest width. The pronotal disc is distinctively more long than broad and tapers more strongly toward the head. Outer lobes of the male supra-anal plate are laterally flattened to a dull point, forming a wide bowl with a bump in the center. The ovipositor is bent at a 90-degree angle and is wider at the base than at the upper portion.

Notes. This is one of the first katydids I had success with identifying by call. Having read Vincent Dethier's *Crickets and Katydids, Concerts and Solos*, I was determined to identify as many species as I could from the keys in his book. On my very first night out I easily heard, and then located the sources of, the many "tzips" in my backyard. From then on, I was hooked!

This is a common species and may very well be the first one you find.

Illustration on page 65.

Treetop Bush Katydid   *Scudderia fasciata*

Range. Canada and south to western South Carolina.

Habitat. The crowns of a variety of conifers, and, to a lesser extent, deciduous trees.

Size. $1^3/8$ to $1^1/2$ inches

Description. Deep green with a pale yellow stripe along the lateral edges of the prono-tum. A *blackish stripe* runs from the base of the tegmina, along the top and to the tips. *Another black stripe* runs along the main vein.

Male Supra-anal Plate. Large, inflated lobes form a deep U that surrounds the sub-genital plate (nearly identical to Fork-tailed Bush Katydid).

Ovipositor. Bends up gently (over 90 degrees) at a little over a quarter of its length from the base. The base is close to the same width as the middle section. Color is often pink.

Call. A single "tsip" repeated at irregular intervals, sometimes fairly close together, sometimes minutes apart. The call is nearly identical to the Fork-tailed Bush Katy-did. The Treetop Bush Katydid, however, usually calls from the tops of conifers; while Fork-taileds can also call from trees, they tend to be in the understory.

Similar Species. While the male supra-anal plate is nearly identical to that of the Fork-tailed Bush Katydid, the Treetop Bush Katydid is the only species in this range with lateral black stripes on the tegmina.

Notes. There has to be a rebel in every family, and this one's it. While most members of the *Scudderia* feed and live among deciduous trees, this one prefers conifers. It is the Scudderian equivalent of the Pine Tree Cricket, which took a similar path away from its broadleaf-inhabiting brethren. For a long time this was known as the Hemlock Bush Katydid, but the name was changed to reflect the fact that it is not always in hemlocks, or even conifers. It *is* always in the tops of trees, however, even if the tops of those trees are only a few feet off the ground. I still prefer the name Hemlock Bush Katydid, because if there is a bush katydid in a hemlock, it's most likely this one. And the tegmina obviously evolved within the pines, as evi-denced by the long, dark stripes in the wings. This is a pattern frequently associ-ated with conifer-feeding insects.

   Fasciatus, by the way, means "striped," which was another name for this species. Perhaps of the three names this would be the most consistent feature to describe it.

Illustration on page 65.

Curve-tailed Bush Katydid   *Scudderia curvicauda*

Range. Canada and south to Florida.

Habitat. Weedy fields, thickets, forest edges, and meadows.

Size. $1^{1}/_{2}$ to $2^{1}/_{8}$ inches

Description. Deep, rich green with a pale line running along the lateral edges of the pronotal disc. The tegmina run parallel until curving gently up about three-quarters of their length from the base. The wings are about four and a half times longer than wide. The hind femora are often magenta.

Male Supra-anal Plate. The outer lobes form a *shallow V*, are blunt, *dorsally flattened,* and turn away from each other. From above, it looks like a whale's fluke with the tips snipped off.

Ovipositor. Short and bends suddenly upward (but more than 90 degrees) at a point about one-third of its length from the base. This species is named for the sharp bend in the ovipositor, but most of the ovipositors in these genera have a sharp bend. It is of a relatively equal width throughout its length. It is often green with deep purple toward the tip.

Pronotal Disc. Distinctively longer than broad, growing narrower toward the head.

Call. Similar to the Fork-tailed Bush Katydid. The "zips" are slightly less lispy, however, and given in a sequence of three: "zip-zip-zip . . . zip-zip-zip. . . ." There will often be another "zip" or two added to the sequence. It calls from late afternoon and into the night.

Similar Species

Fork-tailed Bush Katydid. See account on page 66.

Texas Bush Katydid. Tegmina longer, five to five and a half times longer than their width. The outer lobes of the male supra-anal plate are laterally flattened to a dull point, forming a wide bowl with a bump in the center. The ovipositor is bent at a 90-degree angle and is wider at that base than the area following the bend.

Notes. There are Highbush Blueberry shrubs in the middle of a meadow in my hometown of Killingworth, Connecticut. This is where the Curve-tailed Bush Katydids reign. The males call "zip-zip-zip . . . zip-zip-zip . . ." from the upper branches. In the lower branches and surrounding vegetation, you can see the females "coming hither." I was describing to a woman how the females would gather around the singing male, *swooning*. Then she swooned, "Ohhh Frannnkiiiieeee!" (Guess you had to see that old chicken cartoon to get it.)

Illustration on page 69.

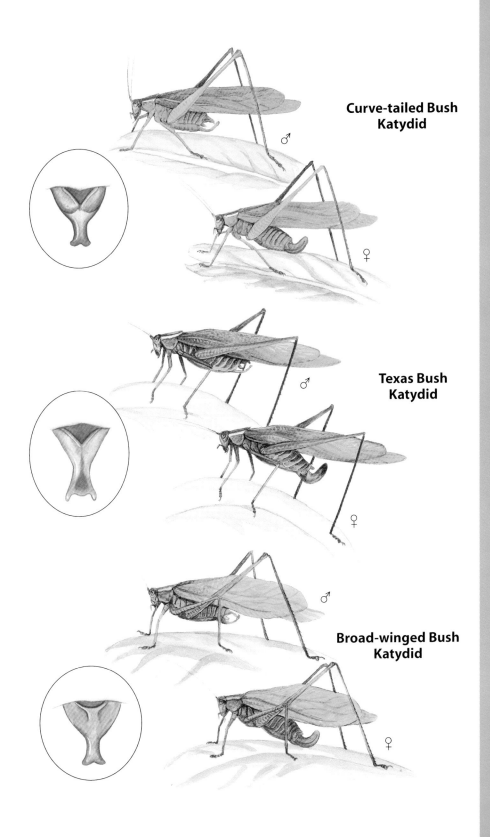

Curve-tailed Bush Katydid

♂

♀

Texas Bush Katydid

♂

♀

Broad-winged Bush Katydid

♂

♀

Range. Canada and south to Florida.

Habitat. Bogs, marshes, wetland edges, meadows, and weedy and grassy fields.

Size. $1^1/_2$ to $2^1/_4$ inches

Description. Grass green, glossy, with a pale yellow line running along the lateral edges of the pronotum. Tegmina are long and narrow, *five to five and a half times* longer than broad. The lower edges of the tegmina bow out slightly just a little past the halfway point from the base. The femora, especially hind ones, can have some brownish red coloration.

Male Supra-anal Plate. Outer lobes are *laterally flattened* to a dull point, forming a wide bowl in between with a bump in the center.

Ovipositor. Broad, more so at the base than the terminal portion. It turns sharply upward with a 90-degree angle at a point about one-third of its length from the base. It is wider at the base than the area following the bend. The edges are often tinged with purple.

Pronotal Disc. Distinctively longer than broad, narrowing toward the head.

Call. This species has three very different calls. One sounds like a very sped up, but quieter, version of a true katydid and is given at night. The individual notes (three or four) merge to sound something like "zi-di-dit." The dusk call consists of a series of wet "ticks" and the day call is a varying train of rapid "zit's." The female also gives a quiet, lispy tick. Calls day and night.

Similar Species

> *Fork-tailed Bush Katydid.* See account on page 66.
> *Curve-tailed Bush Katydid.* See account on page 68.

Notes. Barring the individuals of this species that actually live in Texas, this is by no means a Texas insect. I am not sure where the name came from, but expect it may have had something to do with the origin of the early specimen(s) used to describe it. The name kind of fits, however, because this is one of the largest bush katydids; and as they say, "Everything's big in Texas," right?

Illustration on page 69.

Broad-winged Bush Katydid   *Scudderia pistillata*

Range. Canada and south to West Virginia.

Habitat. Damp and drier meadows, marshes, fields, and roadside thickets.

Size. 1³/₈ to 1³/₄ inches

Description. Grass green with a pale yellow stripe running along the lateral edges of the pronotum. The tegmina are very broad for a bush katydid. There is a noticeable bump, or angle, on the top edge of the wing just before the halfway point from the base. It continues straight from there before angling sharply down to the tip. Along the bottom edge of the wing, there is another less angular, more rounded bulge at about two-thirds the distance from the base of the wing. Then it tapers into a gentle arc toward the tip. The tegmina are strongly veined and are only about *three times long as wide.*

Male Supra-anal Plate. The lobes form a wide, dorsally flattened, rounded V and taper strongly toward the tips. From above it resembles the fluke of a whale.

Ovipositor. Bends up sharply (but slightly more than 90 degrees) at about one-third its length from the base. The middle section and base are of about the same width.

Pronotal Disc. The rear of the disc flares strongly, and steadily, from the front.

Call. This species has three distinct calls. One call begins with a lispy, rapid-sequence "zick-zick-zick." After a pause it adds a slightly louder note or two: "zick-zick-zick-ZICK ZICK." Then another pause and another couple notes are added, those notes louder yet: "zick-zick-zick-zick-zick-ZICK ZICK." It will do this a handful of times before starting over. It also gives a series of crackling, wet "ticks" and a very short, rapid, buzzy "zi-di-dip." Calls day and night.

Similar Species. This is the only species in this genera with an outer wing length only three times its width.

Notes. While Maine misses out on some of the species we enjoy farther south, they are fortunate to have this boreal katydid in their midst. With three different calls, which can be earpiercingly loud, they seem to be filling the void left by the absence of True Katydids.

Illustration on page 69.

True Katydids

Subfamily Pseudophyllinae

True Katydids—Genus *Pterophylla*

The Pseudophyllinae subfamily is a large one (about a thousand species), with four species of this mostly tropical group occurring in North America. There is but one genus in our area, *Pterophylla*, meaning "leaf wing," and it is so unique in appearance and sound, there is little chance of mistaking it for any other species. It is the Common True Katydid.

The members of *Pterophylla* are large, arboreal insects, rarely seen, but surely heard. They inhabit the tops of trees and are most frequently encountered accidentally after being knocked from a tree in a storm. The fact that there is an endless food source (leaves), and other true katydids in neighboring trees, gives them little or no reason to descend from their lofty perches. Another opportunity for seeing them arises, however, when the tallest trees in their vicinity are not much taller than the observer. A true katydid will seek out the highest perch in an area, which may not necessarily be out of your reach.

True katydids have very broad, leaflike tegmina. The tegmina are convex, bulging out at the sides, a unique feature that helps set this group apart. Those tegmina are heavily veined, much like the leaves they dwell upon. The wing shape and vein positioning help amplify the insect's call. In New England, they are the loudest calling Orthoptera. True katydids also have well-developed hind wings hidden beneath the tegmina. Another distinguishing feature is the very long antennae, which are about twice as long as the body. The females have a moderate-lengthed, sickle-shaped ovipositor, which is used to deposit eggs in the loose bark or stems of branches.

Males and females produce calls, the females most likely for the purpose of startling prey. They also respond to the calling males. Most katydids have an alarm call, but the loud, raspy "SCRITCH" given by a male or female true katydid if handled or threatened really gets one's attention. When I was a child I found my first Common True Katydid on the front stoop of my house. I picked it up and it gave that loud call. I was so startled, I immediately dropped it, which, from the katydid's point of view, was exactly how it is supposed to work!

Common True Katydid

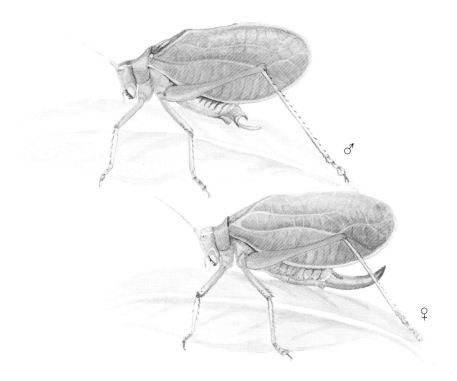

Range. Massachusetts and Vermont, and south to Florida.

Habitat. Crowns of deciduous and coniferous trees, and occasionally in the surrounding shrubs.

Size. 1¹/₂ to 2 inches

Description. Leaf green, legs and body generally paler yellow-green. Tegmina are dull with prominent veins, oval in shape, broad and *noticeably bulging* (convex) on the sides. They completely enclose the abdomen and the inner wings.

In males, the stridulary area is very visible as a brown triangle behind the pronotum. In females, which also can produce sound, the stridulary area is the same color as the rest of the tegmina.

The ovipositor is of moderate length, broad, and curves up to a sharp point. It may either extend past, or be concealed by, the tegmina.

Call. This is the call that gave rise to the name "katydid"; a very loud and repeated, "Tch-tch-tch . . . tch-tch-tch . . . ," which was interpreted as, "kay-ty-did . . . kay-ty-did. . . ." An extra "tch" or two will often be added, especially farther south in their range. True katydids synchronize their calls, dominating the sounds of the summer nights. The call gets deeper, raspier, and slower as the temperature cools, which the illustrator of this book interpreted as, "I'm . . . still . . . here. . . . How . . . 'bout . . . you?" They call primarily at night.

Similar Species. No other katydid in this region has strongly bulging tegmina.

Notes. Another common name for this species is Northern True Katydid. This makes reference to the fact that it is the northernmost occurring katydid of its kin. Recognizing, however, that this species occurs south to Florida, I feel it is more suitable, as do many orthopterists, to call it Common True Katydid, which better defines it within its North American range.

Illustration on page 73.

Shield-backed Katydids
Subfamily Tettigoniinae

The subfamily name Tettigoniinae is an echo of the name from the family in which it rests, Tettigonii**dae**. The name refers to the angled tegmina of the family, which, in the case of this subfamily, does not offer much help in identifying it.

The common name of shield-backed katydid, however, is far more descriptive. They're also known as shield-bearers and, because of their omnivorous nature, as predatory katydids. The katydids in this subfamily share an overlarge pronotum, many appearing as if they're carrying a shield on their back. They are stocky, robust insects, and with their rounded backs, somewhat buffalo or rhinolike in their stance.

There are two wing forms in this subfamily: long-winged and short-winged. Some of the females lack wings entirely.

The shield-backs tend to stay low to the ground, which would explain their mostly brownish, dead-leaf coloration. They feed on a variety of food: leaves, flowers, fruit, and other insects. Eggs are laid in the soil via their stout, straight ovipositors.

Their calls vary widely (because there are so many of them), but tend to be somewhat lisping and buzzy.

Eastern Shieldbacks—Genus *Atlanticus*

Samuel Scudder, noting that this genus was confined to the "Atlantic slope of North America," named it for that region. "Atlantic Shieldback," however, may suggest a seafaring katydid, so the common name for the genus is now Eastern Shieldback.

This genus is much as described in the subfamily treatment. They are creatures of the woodland understory, colored like the dead leaves they traverse—warm browns, reddish browns, and ochre, with black specking. They are highly omnivorous, feeding on grasses, sedges, mushrooms, leaves, flowers, and fruit. They are also successful predators and will capture and eat a wide variety of Arthropods, including field crickets, stinkbugs, caterpillars, and aphids. An injured or weak Eastern Shieldback risks becoming a meal for a healthy relative.

What stands out in these insects is the large pronotal disc, which flares out toward the rear. Also quite noticeable is the boxy shape of the abdomen. The male tegmina are very short and the stridulary organ is either largely or entirely concealed beneath the pronotum. In females, the tegmina are completely hidden, and in both sexes, the hind wings are only vestigial, so they don't fly.

The female ovipositor ranges in length, but is usually fairly long, straight, and either upcurved, or slightly downcurved.

The calls of Eastern Shieldbacks tend to be sputtery and buzzy, often given in short sequences.

Range. Massachusetts and south to Georgia.

Habitat. Low along the edges of woodland trails; borders of thickets.

Size. $^3/_4$ to 1 inch

Body Features. Very robust. The upper face of the pronotum is long, the rear section flaring outward. The dorsolateral ridges of the pronotum are strongly ridged. The male tegmina are *at least as long* as the widest section of the upper pronotum. Females lack visible tegmina.

Color. Overall grayish brown to reddish brown with pale and dark brown speckling. The sides (lobes) of the pronotum are nearly filled with brown-black, but this can be variable. Black blotches fill the sides of the tegmina.

Ovipositor. Longer than the body; broad, straight, and wider at the base. It has a *slight* bulge at upper edge of base, and a *barely discernible* bulge at the lower edge of base.

Call. A lazy series of high, sputtery buzzes, varying in length and broken with irregular intervals of silence. Call begins at dusk and goes into the night.

Similar Species

> *American Shieldback.* Nearly identical, but larger. The tegmina length of American Shieldbacks is only about half the width of the widest area of the upper face of the pronotum. The female's ovipositor has a strong bulge on the lower edge at the base, and no bulge on the upper edge of the base.

Notes. My first encounter with this insect was with its song. It was getting dark and I was walking along a trail when I heard "sh-sh-sh-shhhh . . ." repeated over and over from the ground among the dry leaves. This was a new call to me, and while I couldn't place it, I knew it had to be a katydid of some kind. I searched frantically, hoping to find the singer before it got too dark to see. When I came across the shieldback, I kept looking, thinking it was just a locust. I guess I hadn't looked closely enough, because I obviously missed the long antennae! I went home empty-handed, but returned the next night. When I found the same "locust," in the same area, in the vicinity of the same song, I said "What a minute . . . ," and gave it a closer look. Then I saw the long antennae, the instant giveaway for a katydid.

Illustration on page 77.

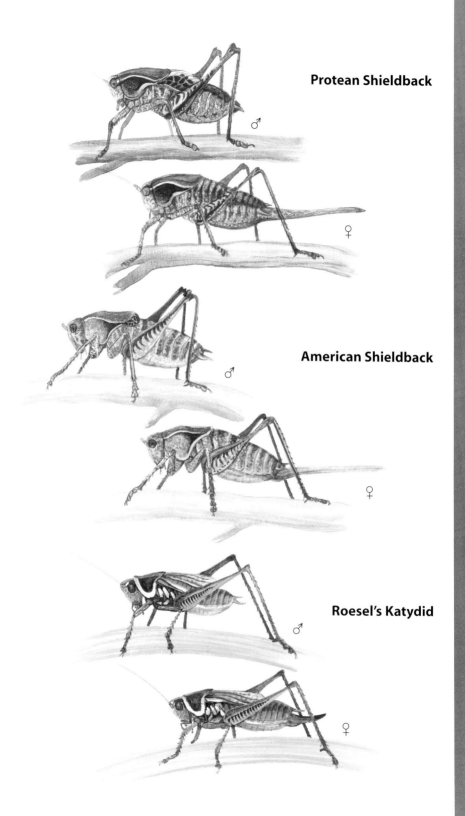

Protean Shieldback

♂

♀

American Shieldback

♂

♀

Roesel's Katydid

♂

♀

Range. Massachusetts and south to Florida.

Habitat. In the undergrowth of deciduous woodlands.

Size. $^7/_8$ to $1^1/_8$ inches

Body Features. Very robust. The upper face of the pronotum is long, the rear section flaring outward. The dorsolateral ridges of the pronotum are strongly keeled. The length of the male tegmina are *about half* the width of the widest section of the pronotal disc. Females lack tegmina.

Color. Overall yellow-brown to reddish brown with pale and dark brown speckling. The sides of the pronotum are partially filled (about one-third) toward the rear with brown-black; however, this can be variable. There is black between the pale veins of the tegmina.

Ovipositor. Longer than the body, broad and straight. There is a *wide* bulge on the lower edge of the base, and *no bulge* on the upper edge of the base, nearly forming a straight line from the upper edge of the base to where it curves down at the tip.

Call. A lazy, but steady, series of high sputtery buzzes. Call begins at dusk and goes into the night.

Similar Species

Protean Shieldback. See account on page 76.

Notes. This was formerly called the "Short-legged Shield-bearer," although the legs only appear short when compared with a Protean Shield-bearer (once known as the "Long-legged Shield-bearer"). This is not a shy insect, and will sing readily in captivity. In fact, it will respond to an imitation of its call. Both shieldbacks are known to give a strong "nip" if handled.

Illustration on page 77.

Genus *Metrioptera*

We have two *Metrioptera* species in North America: *Metrioptera sphagnorum*, Bog Katydid, and *Metrioptera roeselii*, Roesel's Katydid. The former is a Canadian species that nearly makes it to the border of the northern United States, but has not been recorded in this country. The latter made its way to the Northeast from Europe somewhere between the late 1940s and early 1950s.

The *Metrioptera* are medium-sized katydids that range throughout the Old World. They occur in both long-winged and short-winged forms. The female's ovipositor is short, and curves upward. She deposits her eggs in the soft stems of plants.

Our one U.S. species was first discovered in Quebec in 1952. It has since spread south to Long Island, New York. The Long Island species could very well have migrated from Connecticut, as I've come across two of them in my Connecticut yard. As with my first encounter with a shield-backed katydid, Protean Shieldback, my first cursory glance of the insect lead me to believe it was a grasshopper. It was the shape and the heavy pattern that threw me off. Seeing the long antennae, however, immediately dispelled that impression.

Range. Maine and south to New York. Introduced to North America from Europe in the late 1940s/early 1950s.

Habitat. Damp, grassy areas.

Size. $1/2$ to $13/16$ inch

Body Features. Robust; looks like a locust with long antennae. The top of the head is domelike, resembling a bicycle helmet. There are two wing forms. In the long-winged morph, the tegmina extend beyond the tip of the abdomen. In the short-winged morph, the tegmina cover between one-half to four-fifths of the abdomen.

Color. Overall yellow-brown and very *heavily patterned* with black, cream, and green. A double black stripe runs from the top of the head to the end of the pronotal disc. A heavy black area, interrupted with a pale stripe, is over each eye. The lower edge and sides of the pronotum have a heavy white to cream U-shaped border filled with black, and often, green. The tegmina are brown to gray, often with a wash of grass green. The sides of the basal section of the abdomen are marked with white to green oval dots surrounded by black. The legs are yellow to reddish brown and the hind femora have heavy black patterning. The antennae are brown to black.

Ovipositor. Heavy, curved, and projects upward. Usually black with a paler area in the center toward the base.

Call. A sputtering buzz lasting a couple seconds and given at regular intervals. It can also produce a more sustained buzz. Calls mostly during the day and into dusk.

Similar Species. As mentioned, this species would more likely be confused with a locust than another katydid. The long antennae immediately rule that out.

Notes. While not native, *Metrioptera roeselii* is most likely here to stay. Any negative impact of their arrival has yet to be seen. It is an attractive species, and could be the reason it was named for an artist—August Johann Rösel von Rosenhof. Roesel (the "oe" replaces the German use of "ö") was a gifted German painter and naturalist of the 1700s. While he did paint a number of plates depicting crickets and katydids, I was unable to find one of his namesake.

In their native Europe, they are called "Roesel's Bush Crickets."

Illustration on page 77.

Quiet Calling Katydids

(Also known as Long-tailed Katydids and Diurnal Predatory Katydids)

Subfamily Meconematinae

*T*he Meconematinae are a widespread subfamily, with members in Europe, Africa, and Asia. Their common names share the unique attributes to this group: They make little noise (to the human ear); they have very long cerci; they hunt other insects; and they're quite active during the day.

The United States has one species representing this subfamily: *Meconema thalassinum*, or Drumming Katydid. It was introduced from Europe and was first discovered in Long Island, New York, in 1959.

Drumming Katydids—Genus *Meconema*

This little bug has many names: Oak Bush Cricket, Oak Katydid, Drumming Bush Cricket, and Drumming Katydid. Because it was coined from a North American species, "katydid" is a North American name, while "bush cricket" (at least when referring to what we call katydids) belongs to Europe. For this book, I went with the name Drumming Katydid, as it best describes what sets this insect apart from others.

Drumming Katydids inhabit weedy fields, woodland edges, and treetops in deciduous woodlands, often venturing down the bark at night. They are active hunters, catching and feeding on aphids and various leaf and plant hoppers. They also eat a variety of leaves.

Females and males have similar-shaped wings. This is due to the fact that the males lack the visible stridulary apparatus present in most katydids. They do fly, and have been known to be attracted to lights.

The female ovipositor is long, slender, upwardly curved, and is designed for ovipositing within the crevices of bark and beneath the lichen growing on trees.

While many of the Meconematinae are known to stridulate, their call is very quiet, and in some cases, ultrasonic. The Drumming Katydid calls by tapping its hind tarsus on a leaf. The first tarsal segment on the hind tibia is hardened and modified for this purpose.

Range. Massachusetts to southern Long Island (and spreading). Introduced to Long Island from Europe around the early 1950s.

Habitat. Weedy fields, and in and along the borders of deciduous woodlands.

Size. $^3/_8$ to $^3/_4$ inch—our smallest katydid.

Description. *Very small,* sea green (which is the translation of *thalassinum*), with a yellow stripe running down the center of the pronotal disc. The yellow stripe is flanked toward the rear of the thorax by an orange and black dash. Unlike most male katydids, this species show *no distinctive stridulary* area behind the thorax. The wings are long and slender with "cobwebby" veins. The antennae are pale orange.

Male cerci are long, slender, and tubular, curving gently upward. They are often tipped with orange. The female ovipositor is swordlike, not serrated, and curves gently up to a sharp point. It is often tipped with dark red and black.

Call. Lacking a conventional stridulary organ, this species calls by tapping, or "drumming," its hind tarsus on a leaf. Depending upon the amplification qualities of the substrate, the drumming can be heard from a few yards away. Calls at night.

Notes. For a relatively new species to my area, they're certainly plentiful. I find them day and night on trees, shrubs, on my deck, on buildings, and by the porch light. On more than one occasion, I've seen these predators as prey. One of the dangers in crawling around on tree bark at night is coming across a large Wolf Spider, against which this little katydid hasn't a chance.

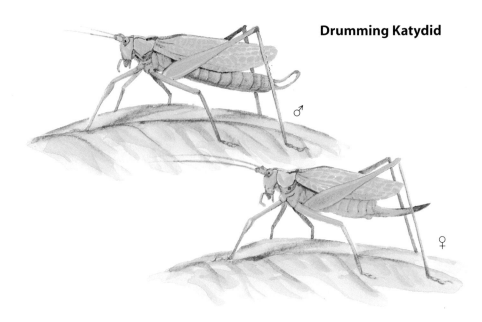

Drumming Katydid

♂

♀

THE MOLE CRICKETS
Family Gryllotalpidae

*T*he European Mole, *Talpa europaea*, is a common subterranean mammal through-out its range. It could be this species, or a relative, whose genus name was added to the Latin root for cricket, "gryllo." *Gryllotalpidae* is essentially "cricket" + "mole."

Mole crickets and moles illustrate a prime example of convergent evolution. You cannot have two life forms much further apart than an insect and a mammal, and yet the adaptive similarities are astounding! While our "mammal-centric" view may lead one to opine that these crickets are just like moles, it is probably more accurate to say the moles are just like these crickets. Insects were here first.

Mole crickets are large, long, robust, and covered in short velvety fur. They live beneath the ground in burrows of their own construction. The burrows are dug with the aid of two highly specialized front legs, the tarsi and tibiae of which form large, blade-like claws, known as *dactyls*.

Their bodies are flattened dorsally, making them better designed for slipping through the soil. Both sexes share an overlarge thorax and a long abdomen with a long pair of cerci extending from the tip. The female ovipositor is either vestigial or absent, and the only way to tell the sexes apart is by the differing vein patterns in the tegmina. Mole crickets have fully functioning hind wings of varying lengths, and females will often fly to the calling males. They are also attracted to lights.

To find these crickets, look for the raised tunnel ridges in the damp soil, sand, or mud along the edges of ponds. The ridges remind me of the Bugs Bunny cartoons I watched as a child. When Bugs traveled beneath the ground, you could follow his route from the surface by the displaced dirt from his tunnel. Some species tunnel beneath grass and other vegetated areas, making them more difficult to locate. Within those tunnels can be special chambers where the females lay their eggs. At the surface, the opening of the tunnel often serves as an amplifier for the calling male, who comes to the very edge to stridulate. The burrow opening works like the acoustic horn of an old Victrola. Some females within this family are also able to stridulate.

These insects feed on a variety of plant roots beneath the ground, and will also eat some of the lower surface foliage. Their diet is supplemented with earthworms, grubs, and other subterranean invertebrates.

There is one native species in our range, the Northern Mole Cricket, and one intro-duced species, the European Mole Cricket. The latter turns up only occasionally and does not seem to have gained a foothold in the Northeast.

Northern Mole Cricket—Genus *Neocurtilla*

Life history is as described on page 83. *Neocurtilla* (and *Gryllotalpa*) have in common four "claws" on the front tibiae. This separates them from the southeastern *Scapteriscus* mole crickets, which only have two claws. The hind tibiae of *Neocurtilla* mole crickets are armed with eight spurs (four inside and four outside). The front femora of those in that genus have a blunt projection, which differs from the sickle-shaped projection borne on the front femora of members in the genus *Gryllotalpa*. *Gryllotalpa* also differ from *Neocurtilla* in the number of spurs present on the hind tibiae; seven, as opposed to eight.

**NORTHERN MOLE CRICKET
FRONT FEMUR**

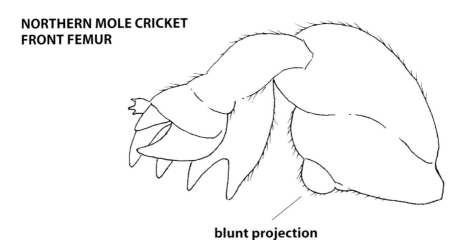

blunt projection

**EUROPEAN MOLE CRICKET
FRONT FEMUR**

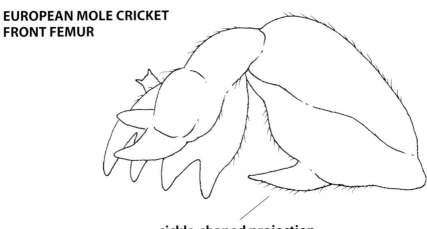

sickle-shaped projection

Range. Maine to Florida.

Habitat. Lives in burrows in damp ground, often along edges of bodies of water.

Size. $3/4$ to $1^1/4$ inches

Description. A robust, medium-sized cricket, with a large thorax and clawed front legs (dactyls). Body is covered in fine, velvety hairs. The tegmina cover about one-half to three-quarters of the abdomen; the fully functional hind wings fall just short of the tip of the abdomen, or greatly exceed it.

Color. Cinnamon to yellow-brown. Washes of brown-black on top of thorax and abdomen. The dark, brown-gray veins on the wings stand out against pale, yellowish base color.

Ovipositor. Vestigial—not visible to naked eye.

Call. It tells you where it lives; a burry "dirt-dirt-dirt. . . ." Mole crickets call from the edges of their burrows, which adds to the resonance of the song. Another description of their call would be "churr-churr-churr . . . ," which gave rise to another of their common names, Chur-worm.

Similar Species

European Mole Cricket, Gryllotalpa gryllotalpa *[not shown].* European Mole Crickets are greater than $1^3/8$ inches long (beyond the greatest length of a Northern Mole Cricket). The front "claw" of the European Mole Cricket has a *sickle-shaped* projection. In the Northern Mole Cricket, that projection is *short and blunt* (see line drawing comparison). From the top, the head and thorax appear egg shaped in the European Mole Cricket. In our native mole cricket, the head and thorax form a teardrop shape.

The Northern Mole Cricket is far more common and far more likely encountered in our range. The European Mole cricket was accidentally introduced to the United States around 1913 (via some plants shipped from Holland to a New Jersey nursery). Its recorded occurrences farther north, however, are sparse.

Notes. Eager to see one of these crickets up close, I built a trap from plans I read about in an orthopterist journal. It was a form of a pitfall trap designed to intercept them as they traveled just below the surface of the mud. The trap worked, but caught only nymphs. So then I grabbed a trowel and started digging in the area of the tunnels, which were obvious by the displaced dirt on the surface. It didn't take long to unearth an adult mole cricket. And then another. And then another. . . . I brought them home and put them in a terrarium filled with the mud from their site. The terrarium was placed in a dark closet in my studio, where they sang every night until I released them back home.

Illustration on page 86.

Northern Mole Cricket

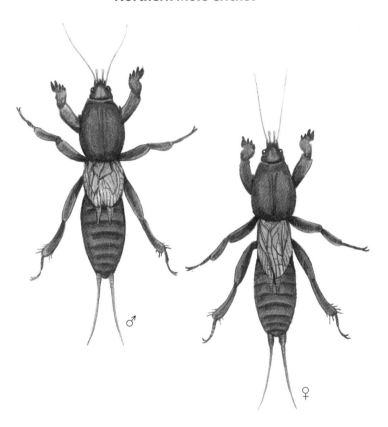

THE TRUE CRICKETS

Family Gryllidae

Since they are primarily ground dwellers (the exception being tree crickets, bush crickets, and trigs), the tegmina of the Gryllidae do not resemble leaves, as do those of the katydids. The upper wings are usually translucent, rest flat on the body, and fold over the sides of the abdomen. In the tree cricket males, the wings just rest flat on the body and do not fold over the sides. Unlike the wing placement in katydids, the right tegmen overlaps the left.

For the most part, the insects are dorsally flattened, designed to hug the ground, branches, and leaves. They tend to be the color of the dead leaves and soil they inhabit. I've always thought of the katydids as the frogs, in their bright greens and pinks and yellows, up in the trees. The crickets are the toads, dark, squat, and on the ground. The tree crickets ruin that analogy, though. They're delicate little stems of green, clinging to the leaves. Of course, some of those shield-bearing katydids are as stout and dark as any field cricket. And then there are the trigs.

That's the problem with this group—they're so diverse. As mentioned earlier in this book, some entomologists place tree crickets and trigs in their own separate families. It's easy to see why.

We do have the three-segmented tarsi to bring them together as a group (the tarsi in katydids are made up of four segments). They also stridulate in a similar fashion. Unlike the katydids, whose outer wings remain close to the body when calling, the crickets lift their tegmina at a sharp angle from their body. As the scraper hits the file, a trill or chirp is produced, generally with more pitch than the song created by the katydids. Individual crickets can produce different sounds. The *call* is used by the male to attract females and to lay claim to territory. The call is a steady, more sustained song than the courtship song. The latter is quieter, more intimate, and used when the male is in close proximity to the female. Many crickets call both day and night, but some call only at night.

The male cricket deposits one or several small spermatophores from the tip of his abdomen onto the tip of the female's. It does not include a spermatophylax for her to feed upon while the sperm is being absorbed. However, she doesn't always go hungry. Some male crickets secrete a nourishing snack for the female via their upper thorax. They lift their wings and allow her to feed while the sperm from the spermatophore is being absorbed. Some crickets provide this meal from a gland at the tip of the abdomen, released only after the spermatophore is in place. And then there are the crickets that offer up their actual wings or tibial spurs (movable spikes on the legs) for the meal.

The arboreal crickets deposit their eggs in the different parts of plants they inhabit—leaves, branches, stems, fruit, and flowers. The ground-dwelling crickets push their eggs into the damp soil. Both forms possess a thin, needlelike ovipositor for this purpose. In some cases, the ovipositor is very long, nearly as long as the cricket. Sometimes, it appears as a tiny spur at the tip of the abdomen.

In the Northeast, the eggs usually overwinter and hatch the following spring. Spring Field Crickets are the exception and overwinter as nymphs. This is why they are they are usually the first insect you hear calling as the nights grow warmer.

As with the katydids, crickets develop through incomplete metamorphosis. There is no larval stage; instead, the nymphs leave the eggs as morphologically similar, but wingless, forms of the adult. They go through five or six molts before reaching the fertile and calling stage.

The cricket diet is quite varied, and they are considered omnivorous. In addition to leafy plant matter, they will feed on detritus (dead insects and animals), live invertebrates, flowers, and fruit. They do well in captivity and many cultures have taken advantage of this, keeping them as pets for their song, or fighting them like pit bulls.

The crickets tend to outlast the katydids into the colder months. This is due to the ability of the smaller, ground-dwelling species to seek out slightly warmer microclimates in the soil. Well after the killing frosts have silenced the woodland edges, there is a chance you'll hear a weak, stuttery trill from the edges of your lawn on a sunny autumn afternoon. That would be the Carolina Ground Cricket, one of the last singers heard before the fields and forest are void of insect song.

Field Crickets
and House Crickets
Subfamily Gryllinae

*F*ield crickets are what come to mind when one thinks of crickets. They are medium to large; robust; dark browns, ochres, and black; live on the ground beneath leaves, rocks, and logs; chirp.

The subfamily that Gryllinae would most easily be confused with is Nemobiinae, or the ground crickets, which at a quick glance will look like a small field cricket. They are best separated from this group by the following:

- Gryllinae lack prominent bristles. Nemobiinae are bristly.
- Gryllinae ovipositors have a smooth, untoothed tip. Nemobiinae ovipositor tip is bumpy or toothed.
- Gryllinae hind tibiae have short, inflexible spines (less than the width of the tibia). Nemobiinae hind tibiae have long flexible tibial spurs (considerably greater in length than the width of the hind tibia).
- Gryllinae are big, generally greater than one-half inch long. Nemobiinae are small, less than one-half inch long.

The field crickets are so named for their preference of habitat. They prefer the leafy edges of woodlands where they spend most of their time beneath ground-hugging shelters. Their calls are loud and rich, and are given from the edges of their shelters and burrows.

Four genera and six species of Gryllinae are included in this book. Two of those species, *Acheta domesticus* (House Cricket) and *Velarifictorus micado* (Japanese Burrowing Cricket), are introduced. While not called field crickets, they are members of Gryllinae, as they share the morphological characteristics of this subfamily.

Fall Field Cricket / Spring Field Cricket
Gryllus pennsylvanicus / Gryllus veletis

Range. *Fall Field Cricket.* Maine and veering west to Texas from South Carolina.

Spring Field Cricket. Maine to North Carolina.

Habitat. Occurs in grassy areas, beneath leaves, logs, and rocks; along edges of woods and yards.

Size. $^5/_8$ to $^7/_8$ inch

Description. Among the larger of the crickets in our range; broad, with a barrel-shaped body. From the top, the head is just slightly wider than the width of the pronotum. In males, the tegmina nearly reach the tip of the abdomen. In females, the tegmina cover about four-fifths of the abdomen. Wings are usually hidden beneath the tegmina, but sometimes they extend beyond the tip of the abdomen. The upper face and the side of the pronotum lack bristles.

Morphologically, the Spring Field Cricket is virtually indistinguishable from the Fall Field Cricket. They are best separated by the time of year they occur as adults. The Spring Field Crickets reach maturity April through July. The Fall Field Crickets occur as adults from August through the first few frosts. There can be an overlap of the two species from late July to early August.

Color. The head, body, and legs are *shiny and black* with no distinguishable markings. The tegmina and cerci range from light brown to black. In some cases the veins in the sides of the wings are yellow-brown.

Ovipositor. *Nearly as long as the length of the abdomen,* projecting up from the base. The ovipositors of Fall Field Crickets average $^5/_8$ inch, while in the Spring Field Crickets they fall short of that length.

Call. The calls of the Fall and Spring Field Crickets are to the crickets what the call of the True Katydid is to the katydids. It is the sound most associated with that entire family. In the case of the field crickets, it's a rich, loud "chirp . . . chirp . . . chirp. . . ."

Similar Species

Sand Field Cricket. While similar to Spring and Fall Field Crickets in size and form, Sand Field Crickets are overall larger, although there is an overlap between the largest Fall Field Crickets and the smaller Sand Field Crickets. If you have a female, check the ovipositor length. The shortest length of the ovipositor of Sand Field Cricket is $^3/_4$ inch, the average being $^7/_8$ inch, and it tends to exceed the length of the body. Three-quarters of an inch is the maximum length of the Fall Field Cricket's ovipositor, which averages about $^5/_8$ inch, and falls short of the length of the body.

The tegmina of Sand Field Crickets are generally more yellow to reddish brown and stand out more in contrast to the body.

The call is slightly lower in pitch than that of the Spring and Fall Field Crickets.

Lastly, a field cricket along the coast from Virginia to Florida is far more likely to be a Sand Field Cricket since the Fall and Spring Field Crickets do not occur in this area.

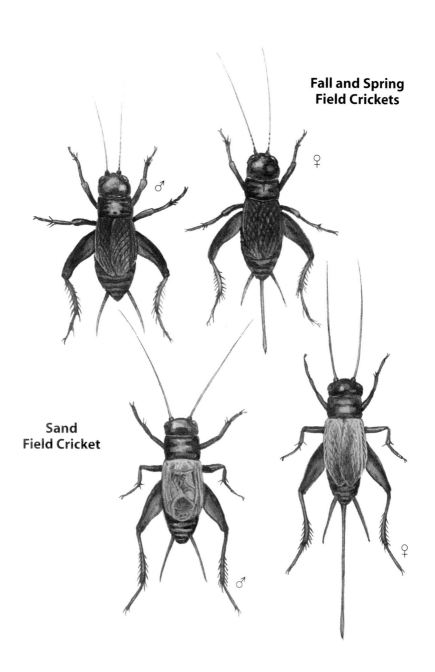

Fall and Spring Field Crickets

♂

♀

Sand Field Cricket

♂

♀

Notes. From late April to July, we hear the Spring Field Crickets chirping outside our bedroom windows. Then, from early August to November, the Fall Field Crickets take their place. They call all day and into the night. You listen to them as you fall asleep and wonder if they ever take a break. Come morning, though, they are silent. This is when the crickets give their hard-working tegmina a well-earned rest.

There is another break in the field cricket calls, one that most people fail to notice. This takes place during that brief period in time when last year's Spring Field Crickets have crawled under that big leaf in the sky, and this year's Fall Field Cricket nymphs are nearly ready to molt into their adult-singing stage. This period of silence rarely lasts for more than two weeks and it's most noticeable when the singing returns. To catch this period is like catching an eclipse of sound.

For me, this changing of the guard is a marker in time. It is nature taking a breath, and then continuing with renewed vigor.

Illustration on page 91.

Sand Field Cricket   *Gryllus firmus*

Range. Connecticut and south to Florida.

Habitat. Beneath cover on beaches and in dry, sandy fields, lawns, and edges of roads.

Size. $^3/_4$ to $1^1/_8$ inches

Description. Very robust. From the top, the head is just slightly wider than the width of the pronotum. In males, the tegmina range from covering three-quarters to the entire abdomen. In females, they cover three-quarters to seven-eighths of the abdomen. Hind wings are usually hidden beneath the tegmina, but sometimes they extend beyond the tip of the abdomen. The face and sides of the pronotum lack bristles.

Color. The head and body are shiny and black with no distinguishable markings. The tegmina and cerci range from yellow-brown to black, but in most species are pale, *yellowish brown.* The veins on the sides of the wings are yellowish, and are noticeably paler than the body.

Ovipositor. Usually *longer* than the length of the abdomen; projecting up from the base.

Call. A rich "churp . . . churp . . . churp," similar to that of the Fall and Spring Field Crickets, but slightly deeper in pitch.

Similar Species

   Fall and Spring Field Crickets. See account on pages 90 and 92.

Notes. Turn over a log on a beach and if there are crickets under it, they will most likely be this species. At first glance they appear like pale-winged Fall Field Crickets, but if one happens to be a female, there will be little question that it's a Sand Field Cricket. While the tegmina of *firmus* are undoubtedly paler (and more yellow) than *pennsylvanicus*, the ovipositors are extremely long.

   Where you run into trouble is with the hybrids. Fall and Sand Field Crickets are known to interbreed.

Illustration on page 91.

Range. New Jersey and south to Florida.

Habitat. Dry, wooded areas beneath stones, leaves, and logs.

Size. $^3/_8$ to $^5/_8$ inch

Description. Fairly small for a field cricket. The head appears *large in comparison to the body*. The tegmina of the male cover about one-half to three-quarters of the abdomen. In the female they cover about one-third to one-half the abdomen. Hind wings are hidden beneath the tegmina. The face and the side of the pronotum lack bristles.

Color. The top of the head is black with short, very faint stripes emanating from the front, dorsal edge of the pronotum. Cheeks and mandibles are ivory white to pale yellow. Pale yellow borders the eyes and the top of the antennal bases. The tegmina are dark brown, suffused with pale yellow. Top of the abdomen often has a dark, straw-bordered stripe down the center. The legs and cerci range from pale yellow to gray-brown.

Ovipositor. Straight, projecting at a slight upward angle and about the length of the abdomen.

Call. A slow "zeet?" given at intervals of several seconds.

Similar Species

Fall, Spring, and Sand Field Crickets. These three species lack the pale patterns in the face and head. Their mandibles are black, unlike the pale mandibles of the Eastern Striped Cricket. From the top, the head is not much wider than the pronotum, as opposed to the Eastern Striped Cricket's seemingly large head. The Eastern Striped Cricket should not be found north of New Jersey.

Japanese Burrowing Cricket. Both species have a strongly patterned head and face, but the Japanese Burrowing Cricket lacks the heavy, pale border around the lower part of the eye. Also, in the Japanese Burrowing Cricket, there is a thin, but distinctive, wide inverted V between the two eyes. It is not nearly as distinctive in the Eastern Striped Cricket. From the top, the former's head is only slightly wider than the pronotum, whereas the head of the Eastern Striped Cricket is considerably wider than the pronotum.

House Cricket. Both species have a strongly patterned head and face, but the House Cricket is the only species with four pale, heavy bars running from eye to eye. From the top, the head is only slightly wider than the thorax.

Notes. *Mio* means "less" or "smaller." *Gryllus* means "cricket." *Saussurei* is the honorific name for Henri Louis Frédéric de Saussure. So this is, in essence, Henri Saussure's Smaller Field Cricket. Saussure was a Swiss hymenopterist and orthopterist who first described the genus *Miogryllus* in 1877. His name is attached to many species of the Orthoptera.

Illustration on page 95.

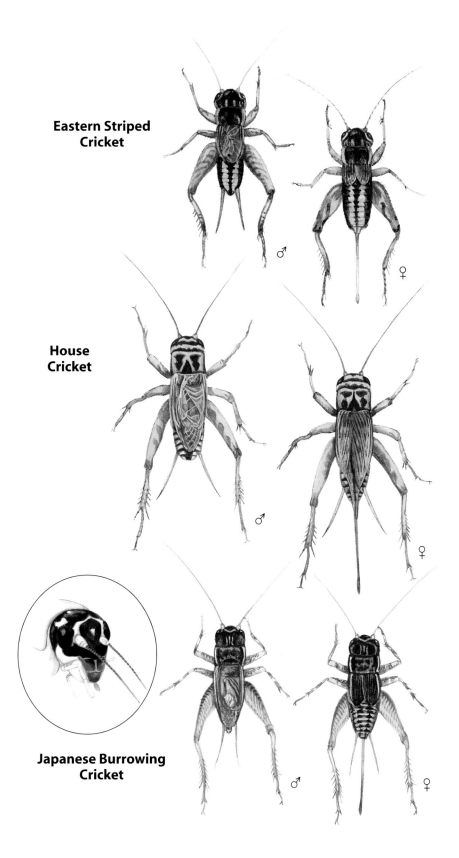

**Eastern Striped
Cricket**

♂

♀

**House
Cricket**

♂

♀

**Japanese Burrowing
Cricket**

♂

♀

House Cricket   *Acheta domesticus*

Range. Maine to Florida. This is an Old World species introduced to the United States.

Habitat. In warm weather, they can be found outdoors in the vicinity of buildings. They cannot survive the winter cold, so when the weather cools, they seek the shelter of heated dwellings, where they inhabit warm, dark places usually on the ground floor and in basements.

Size. $^5/_8$ to $^3/_4$ inch

Description. Slender; looking from above, the head is just slightly wider than the width of pronotum. The tegmina of males and females cover two-thirds to the entire abdomen. The hind wings are either covered by the tegmina, or extend well past the abdomen, coming to a point.

Color. Overall straw colored, with dark brown markings. The head has *four dark brown bars:* one along the top, front edge of the pronotum; one between the eyes; one between the antennae; and one across the "mouth."

Ovipositor. Long, upward tilting, shorter than the length of the abdomen.

Call. A high, rich, burry "cheerp . . . cheerp . . . cheerp. . . ."

Similar Species

Eastern Striped Cricket. See account on page 94.

Notes. If you want to see this cricket, go to a pet store. This is the species most often sold as live food for pet lizards and snakes. In fact, you won't even have to buy them to see them, because they will be in the tanks displaying the reptiles for sale. They are also used for fishing bait. That is their lot in life here in America—raised to be fed to others.

Some of these insects do live out better lives in our homes and buildings, and in the past they were given the endearing term "Cricket on the hearth." Hearing a chirping cricket on the hearth was supposed to presage good luck. However, we don't see a lot of them anymore. Perhaps this is due to the advances in building techniques, which better allow us to keep outdoors those things we wish to keep outdoors.

Illustration on page 95.

Japanese Burrowing Cricket   *Velarifictorus micado*

Range. New Jersey to Florida. Introduced from Asia to the United States in the 1950s.

Habitat. Cosmopolitan: grassy edges of fields and woods, edges of freshwater wetlands. Calls from mouth of its burrow.

Size. $^1/_2$ to $^7/_8$ inch

Description. Fairly small for a field cricket. The head is not much wider than the pronotum. The tegmina in males cover three-quarters to nearly the entire abdomen. In females they cover about half the abdomen.

Color. Overall body is a pale, yellowish gray to deep brown. Underside is paler than dorsal area. The top of the pronotum has pale speckling. Tegmina are dark brown and can have a pale, yellowish stripe on the dorsolateral edge, and a pale yellow wash on the lower lateral edge. The legs are pale straw colored, with dark markings and mottling. The hind legs can have reddish knees.

Face is dark with pearly white in the cheeks, between the eyes, and in an inverted triangular spot between the antennae. Above that pale, inverted triangle, is a thin, but *distinctive,* wide inverted V between the two eyes. The palpi are *pearly white.*

Ovipositor. Long, upward tilting, slightly longer than the length of the abdomen.

Call. A series of burry chirps: "cheer-cheer-cheer . . . ," strung closely together. It is similar to that of the *Gryllus* species, but the call is more rapid. The males call from the opening of their burrow, which offers them a quick escape.

Similar Species

Eastern Striped Cricket. See account on page 94.

Notes. I first came across these crickets at the Altona Marsh Nature Conservancy Easement property in West Virginia. To access this area, you need to walk along a train track. The Japanese Burrowing Crickets were calling all over the place. But how to catch them? As I walked along the rails, I spotted many field cricket nymphs and picked up a few to rear out. Only one turned out to be *micado*, and it was a female. Weeks later, I found myself in Maryland, where I was able to catch a male. I kept them in my home, as the Chinese have been known to do for centuries, and enjoyed the male's call until he, and his mate, died of old age.

In China, these crickets are known as "Cu Zhi," and are pitted against one another in the sport of cricket fighting.

Illustration on page 95.

Ground Crickets

Subfamily Nemobiinae

These little crickets are everywhere! They're active day and night and fill habitat niches ranging from dry gravel to floating sphagnum bogs. A walk across your lawn will no doubt send them hopping and scurrying away at your advance. A species approaching one-half inch would be a giant among the Nemobiinae.

Ground crickets were once grouped into the Gryllinae subfamily. They have now been assigned their own based upon the features I highlighted in the description of field crickets. Some have taken it further and consider the ground crickets worthy of their own family, the Nemobiidae.

Diminutive as they may be, the Nemobiinae are a hardy species, calling at the onset and closing of the Orthoptera breeding seasons. Their calls are generally high-pitched pulses in the form of a continuous or broken trill. Some males within this sub-family have a gland that produces a special quaff for the female that has chosen him. To access the nutritious meal, the female chews off the tip of a spur on the male's hind tibia. This "opens the cap" and the fluid flows forth.

The ovipositors of this group tend to be more laterally flattened than those of the other Gryllidae. Eggs are laid in the damp soil and overwinter in this stage, although some can hatch sooner and overwinter as nymphs.

The Nemobiinae feed on a wide range of low plants, fallen fruit, and detritus. They are very similar in color (dark red-browns to black) and form, and can be a challenge to separate. However, separating them *can* be accomplished by looking at some key morphological features, such as the shape of the pronotum, color patterns, tibial spurs, and by the often noticeable differences in their calls.

Three genera of Nemobiinae occur in the Northeast United States, all covered in this book. I've used the common names presented by orthopterist Thomas Walker on his Web site "Singing Insects of North America."

Robust Ground Crickets—Genus *Allonemobius*

These are among the larger and easier to identify ground crickets. All of the species within our range are quite common and have calls that are different enough to allow the listener to distinguish one from the other with relative ease.

In some cases, though, it may be necessary to know for certain the cricket you're looking at is an *Allonemobius*. The *Allonemobius* can be separated from the other two ground cricket genera by comparing the length of the two *ventral apical* (also known as *distoventral*) spurs on the hind tibiae, and by the shape and length of the ovipositor. It is the differences in these features that have defined these genera for many decades.

Starting with the spurs—first, you may need a loupe or hand lens. You'll be looking at the ventral apical tibial spurs, which are little bitty things. *Ventral* means underside. *Apical* and *distal* both mean farthest from the base, namely, the tip. So you will be looking at the very tip of the lower surface of the hind tibia. There will be two downward-pointing spurs between that tip and the first segment of the tarsus (foot). Bear in mind they will be surrounded by other longer spurs, but you will only be looking at the two shorter parallel spurs at the tip of the lower surface of the leg. In *Allonemobius*, they are very uneven in length. In *Eunemobius*, they are nearly equal in length, hence the common name "Even-spurred Ground Cricket."

If they are equal in length, and the cricket is within the range covered in this book, it is likely to be a Carolina Ground Cricket. You can go read this species' account on page 111 for more information.

If they are unequal in length, it is either *Allonemobius* or *Neonemobius*. The former tend to be at least three-eighths of an inch long (hence the name "Robust Ground Cricket"), and *Neonemobius* tend to be less than three-eighths of an inch long (hence the name "Small Ground Cricket"). There can be some overlap, however, so it is better to refer to the other individual identification clues when separating these two genera.

If you are in the possession of a female, you may be able to use the ovipositor for further clues. If the ovipositor is more than two-thirds the length of the hind femur, and straight, it's probably a species of *Allonemobius*. If it is less than two-thirds the length of the hind femur and slightly curved, it should be *Neonemobius*.

GROUND CRICKET TIBIAL SPURS

**Allonemobius
and Neonemobius**

Eunemobius

Spotted Ground Cricket   *Allonemobius maculatus*

Range. Southern Connecticut and south to Florida.

Habitat. Leaf litter in dry, open woods and along the edges of thickets.

Size. Averages ³/₈ inch

Description. Medium-sized for the genus. In males, the tegmina cover two-thirds of the abdomen. In females, they cover about one-third. In both sexes, the ends of the tegmina are blunt. No hind wings are present. The pronotum grows slightly narrower toward the head and is somewhat bristly.

Color. Overall pale brown, *mottled with dark spots* (hence the name). The eyes are rimmed with a thin band of yellow, giving the impression of spectacles. The rest of the face and head are strongly mottled. A thin yellow band runs along the dorsolateral and hind ridge of the tegmina.

Ovipositor. Straight and nearly reaches the length of the hind femur.

Call. A very high, fast, pulsing, and burry trill—"ti-ti-ti-ti. . . ."

Similar Species

Allard's and Tinkling Ground Crickets. Both lack the heavy mottling in the head and body. The tips of the tegmina are slightly rounded, as opposed to squared off.

Striped and Southern Ground Crickets. Considerably larger than the Spotted Ground Cricket. Top of head has distinct pale stripes, not present in Spotted Ground Crickets. The pronotum is barrel-shaped, as opposed to Spotted's, which gets narrower toward the front.

Notes. These are not very common within the range covered in this book, but they're here. This is a handsome cricket that could easily be passed over as just one of the "regular" ground crickets, until you have a closer look. The mottling and spectacles are a good clue to its identification.

Illustration on page 101.

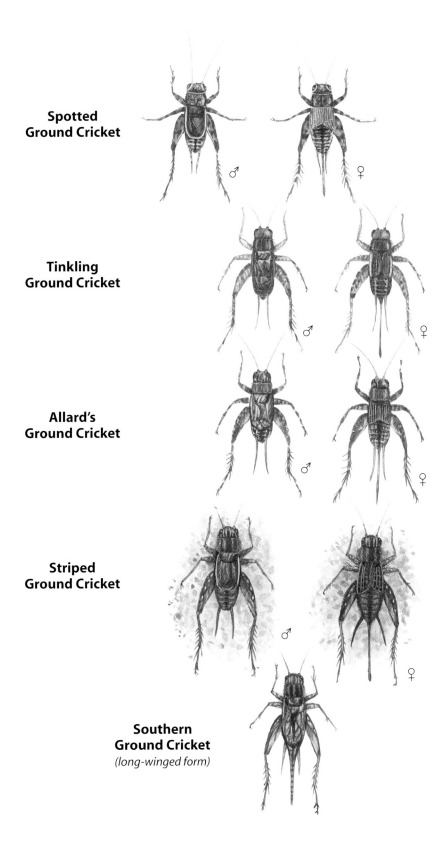

Spotted Ground Cricket ♂ ♀

Tinkling Ground Cricket ♂ ♀

Allard's Ground Cricket ♂ ♀

Striped Ground Cricket ♂ ♀

Southern Ground Cricket
(long-winged form)

Tinkling Ground Cricket   *Allonemobius tinnulus*

Range. New Hampshire and south to Texas.

Habitat. In leaf litter along dry, sunny edges of woods and fields.

Size. Averages $3/8$ inch

Description. Medium-sized for the genus. In males, the tegmina cover three-quarters to seven-eighths of the abdomen. In females, they cover about one-half to five-eighths. In both sexes, the ends of the tegmina are blunt, but slightly rounded. In females, they form a wide, rounded, shallow W. Hind wings are very short. The pronotum grows slightly narrower toward the head and is somewhat bristly.

Color. Overall pale, buffy gray to reddish brown. Head is very often *orange and lacks distinctive markings.* The pronotum can also be infused with deep orange. In females, there can be a dark stripe, surrounded by a buffy border, running laterally down the top of the abdomen.

Ovipositor. Straight, projecting up at an angle. The length is slightly greater than the length of the hind femur.

Call. A steady train of "tink-tink-tink." The tinks are faster and closer together in warm weather and may resemble the trill of a slower-calling Allard's Ground Cricket. In Tinkling Ground Cricket, however, you can always make out the individual "tink." In Allard's, the notes run together to create a trill, although a slow-calling Allard's can make you throw your hands up in defeat. One clue is the habitat. Allard's are in more grassy areas, whereas Tinkling Ground Crickets are in dry, sunny, oak woodland areas.

Similar Species

Allard's Ground Cricket. The head and pronotum are orange-brown in the Tinkling Ground Cricket. In Allard's, they are dark brown with faint lateral stripes on top.

Striped and Southern Ground Crickets. Larger; top of head has distinctive pale stripes on a dark background, as opposed to the somewhat clean, dark orange head of the Tinkling Ground Cricket. The pronotum is barrel shaped, as opposed to that of the Tinkling Ground Cricket, which gets narrower toward the front. Southern Ground Cricket's northern range limit is New Jersey.

Notes. Of all the crickets, this is the one people find easiest to remember. Once the call is pointed out to them, along with the matching name, a look of understanding crosses their faces. Although to me, the call is more of a "tink" than a "tinkle" (which has another connotation). The species name, *tinnulus*, comes from the Latin *tinnire*, which means "sound like a bell." The call can be likened to the steady striking of a tiny bell.

Illustration on page 101.

Range. Maine and south to Georgia.

Habitat. Lawns and other grassy areas; woodland edges.

Size. Averages ³/₈ inch

Description. Medium-sized for the genus. In males, the tegmina cover two-thirds to seven-eighths of the abdomen. In females, they cover about one-third to three-eighths. In both sexes, the ends of the tegmina are blunt, but slightly rounded. In females they form a wide, rounded, shallow W. Hind wings are very short. The pronotum grows slightly narrower toward the head and is somewhat bristly.

Color. Overall dark reddish brown to black. Head is dark, same color as body and often bears *very faint pale stripes* running from back to front of the top of the head.

Ovipositor. Straight, projecting up at an angle. The length is slightly greater than the length of the hind femur.

Call. A high-pitched, continuous trill. There is a pulsing quality to the call. See the Tinkling Ground Cricket call description above for comparison.

Similar Species

Tinkling Ground Cricket and Spotted Ground Cricket. See accounts on pages 100 and 102.

Striped and Southern Ground Crickets. Larger: top of head has distinctive pale stripes on a dark background. In Allard's Ground Cricket the stripes are either lacking or very faint. The pronotum is barrel shaped in Striped and Southern Ground Crickets, as opposed to that in the Allard's Ground Cricket, which gets narrower toward the front. Southern Ground Cricket's northern range limit is New Jersey.

Notes. Harry A. Allard (1880–1963) was a Massachusetts-born botanist, ornithologist, and entomologist. He made his big splash in the science world with his discovery of photoperiodism, the law governing the blossoming and fruiting of plants. He also studied the songs of insects—how they made them, why they made them, and who was making them. This earned him the honorific naming of a very common, and most welcomed singer throughout our region.

Illustration on page 101.

Striped Ground Cricket   *Allonemobius fasciatus*

Range. Maine and south to Virginia.

Habitat. Found in a variety of wet and dry sandy habitats. Often along edges of rivers, ponds, and marshes.

Size. Averages $1/2$ inch

Description. Largest ground cricket in our area. There are two wing forms. In the short-winged form, the tegmina of the male covers about two-thirds of the abdomen. In the female, they cover about half. In both the male and female, the hind wings are hidden beneath them. In the long-winged form, the hind wings come to a point well beyond the tip of the abdomen. The pronotum is *barrel shaped* and, along with the head, densely covered with short, bristly hairs. The head appears to be bulging out of the top of the pronotum and is close to it in width.

Color. Rusty brown to black; tegmina and head are usually lighter in color than the body. The top of the head has *four or five orangey lateral stripes* (hence the name *fasciatus,* meaning striped). The sides of the pronotum are buffy, with a heavy dark bar running front to back. The sides of the tegmina are somewhat lighter in color, with that dark bar from the pronotum continuing through and ending at the rear of the tegmina.

Ovipositor. Fairly straight, curves slightly upward. The length is slightly greater than the length of the hind femur.

Call. A high, burry "chit . . . chit . . . chit. . . ."

Similar Species

Southern Ground Cricket, Allonemobius socius, [*not shown*]. Indistinguishable from the closely related Striped Ground Cricket and best separated by range. The northernmost range of Southern Ground Cricket is southern New Jersey. The southernmost range of Striped Ground Cricket is northern Virginia. All other characteristics of this species are as described in the Striped Ground Cricket account.

Gray Ground Cricket. See account on page 105.

Notes. I used to associate this species with wetlands, as they are ever-present in salt marshes, fens, bogs, and edges of rivers and lakes. I was in a friend's yard, however, which does not fit into any of those habitat categories, and observed an abundance of these crickets. Then I noticed the ground—it was sand. About twenty years prior, he had spread sand over his property to create a riding ring for his horses.

So, it's the sand they like!

Illustration on page 101.

Gray Ground Cricket   *Allonemobius griseus*

Range. Maine and south to South Carolina.

Habitat. Sandy and gravelly areas with sparse vegetation.

Size. Averages $^3/_8$ inch

Description. Small; head bulges slightly from the front of the pronotum, the two nearly equal in width. The pronotum is slightly narrower toward the front. In females, the tegmina cover about half of the abdomen. In males, the tegmina cover about three-quarters of the abdomen. The tegmina tips are broad and slightly rounded.

Color. The face is black or very dark brown and can contrast with the top of the head, which has three black stripes running front to back. The body is gray above and darker gray to black along the sides. The body and wings are covered with *short, gray fur,* giving it a paler appearance.

Ovipositor. Straight, projecting up at an angle. The length is slightly greater than the length of the hind femur.

Call. Soft, high-pitched, somewhat sputtery trill. Calls day and night.

Similar Species

Striped and Southern Ground Crickets. While these two species share heavy stripes on the top of the head, they are both considerably larger and not as bristly.

Notes. Few crickets in our area can take advantage of the dry habitats this species calls home. The Sand Field Cricket is one, although they are usually not very far from water. The most noticeable feature of the Gray Ground Cricket is the long, bristly fur. My guess is it is an adaptation to its habitat, which allows it to retain moisture.

Gray
Ground Cricket

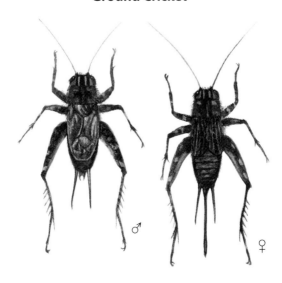

Small Ground Crickets—Genus *Neonemobius*

These tiny ground crickets have a long history of being confused with other small Nemobiinae, including the Carolina Ground Cricket. They share the *Allonemobius* feature of apical spurs of unequal length, but are smaller (less than three-eighths of an inch) than members of that genus. While the tiny Carolina Ground Cricket (*Eunemobius* genus) has apical spurs of equal length, they can also be separated by a difference in the tip of the ovipositor. In the Carolina Ground Cricket, and other *Eunemobius* species, the tip of the ovipositor has heavy teeth above and short teeth below. A *Neonemobius* ovipositor tip has fine teeth above and no teeth below.

Range. Connecticut and south to Florida.

Habitat. The base of tall grasses and sedges in wetland areas.

Size. $^3/_{16}$ to $^5/_{16}$ inch

Description. Very small. The tegmina in males cover seven-eighths to the whole abdomen. In females, they cover two-thirds to the entire length of the abdomen. The tips of the tegmina are broadly rounded and sometimes cover the hind wings. More frequently, however, the hind wings are about double the length of the tegmina and extend well past the abdomen. The pronotum is slightly narrowed toward the head, which is about the same width. The head and pronotum are scattered with long, bristly black hairs.

Color. Overall rusty brown to black, the top of the abdomen is black with rows of *yellowish spots* along the "spine." The tegmina are dark brown to black, often with yellowish markings. In females, the tegmina have short, *yellowish crossveins* toward the outer dorsal edge. A buffy stripe runs along the length of the dorsolateral ridge. The top of the head and pronotum are dark, often with buffy dots.

Ovipositor. Nearly straight and slightly curved upward; considerably shorter than the hind femur.

Call. A high-pitched trill. Calls day and night.

Similar Species

Sphagnum Ground Cricket. Very similar in size and shape, but while most Cuban Ground Crickets have long wings projecting twice the length of the tegmina, the hind wings are not visible in Sphagnum Ground Crickets. The male tegmina in the former cover from seven-eighths to the entire abdomen. In the latter, they cover about three-quarters. The female tegmina in *cubensis* cover from two-thirds to the entire abdomen. In *palustris*, they cover up to one-half. Looking from the top, the pronotum of Cuban Ground Crickets tapers toward the front. In Sphagnum Ground Crickets, the sides are nearly parallel. Sphagnum Ground Crickets lack the yellow markings present in Cuban Ground Crickets and are restricted to open sphagnum bogs.

Notes. The name suggests that this is an introduced species, from Cuba. Its first description, however, by French entomologist Henri De Saussure in 1849, came from a specimen collected in Cuba. This is largely a southern species and far less common in the Northeast than the similar-sounding Carolina Ground Cricket.

Illustration on page 108.

Cuban Ground
Cricket

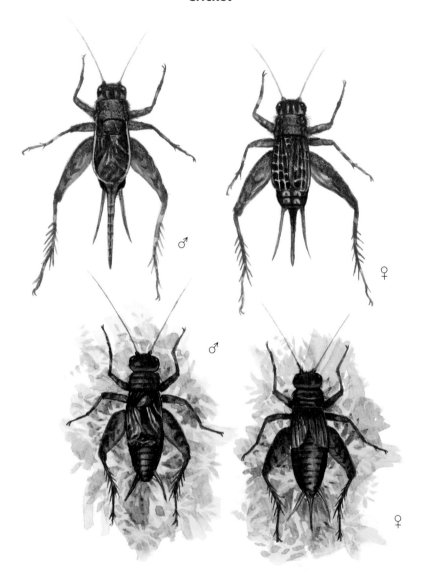

♂

♀

♂

♀

Sphagnum Ground
Cricket

Sphagnum Ground Cricket
Neonemobius palustris

Range. Maine and south to Florida.

Habitat. Open sphagnum bogs.

Size. $^3/_{16}$ to $^1/_4$ inch

Description. This is our smallest ground cricket. The tegmina in males cover about three-quarters of the abdomen. In females, they cover about half the abdomen. The tips of the tegmina are broadly rounded and completely cover the hind wings. The sides of the pronotum are nearly parallel. The head and pronotum are scattered with long, bristly black hairs.

Color. While highly variable, the color is usually *unbroken by spots or patterns.* They are overall uniformly dark brown to black, although sometimes pale yellow-brown. The head and pronotum are often reddish brown. The legs are orange to yellow-brown, and usually paler than the body.

Ovipositor. Slightly bowed and gently curved upward; considerably shorter than the hind femur.

Call. A series of high, feeble trills, lasting several seconds. When combined with other singing males in the bog, however, the trill sounds continuous. Calls day and night.

Similar Species

Cuban Ground Cricket. See account on page 107.

Carolina Ground Cricket. See *Eunemobius* genus account on page 110 for physical differences. While Carolina Ground Crickets will be found in clumps of sphagnum moss, they do not inhabit open sphagnum bogs. Note too the difference in the apical spurs on the tibiae and the tips of the ovipositor, as described in the *Eunemobius* genus account.

Notes. The search for these crickets brought me to my first quaking bog. It was part of The Nature Conservancy's holdings in the northwest corner in Connecticut, and I had received permission to look for them. It didn't take long to find them. The combined calls of the many individual males created a gentle, ethereal trill over this primitive habitat. The crickets were easily captured by slogging into the bog and pressing down into the sphagnum moss with both hands. This flooded the small area, sending the crickets scurrying to the surface.

Illustration on page 108.

Even-spurred Ground Crickets—Genus *Eunemobius*

The *Eunemobius* crickets are small, somewhat slender, and the females possess a short, slightly upwardly curved ovipositor. They are separated by the other two northeastern genera of ground crickets by the ventral apical spurs,* which are of even length. In the other genera, they are of uneven length. The ovipositor is also different, the tip having heavy teeth above and short teeth below. In the *Allonemobius* and *Neonemobius* crickets, the tip of the ovipositor only has fine teeth above.

---

* A description of the differences is in the Robust Ground Cricket account on pages 98 to 99.

Carolina Ground Cricket

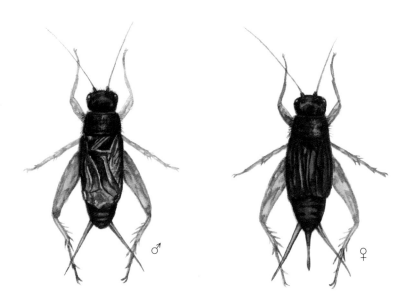

♂   ♀

Carolina Ground Cricket   *Eunemobius carolinus*

Range. Maine and south to Florida.

Habitat. In leaf litter along woodland edges; fields, lawns, borders of streams and ponds.

Size. $^3/_{16}$ to $^5/_{16}$ inch

Description. Small; somewhat flattened. The tegmina in males cover about three-quarters to seven-eighths of the abdomen. In females, they cover about two-thirds of the abdomen. The tips of the tegmina are bluntly pointed and cover the hind wings. The sides of the pronotum narrow toward the front; the head is wider than the front of the pronotum, giving it a more prominent appearance. The *palpi are whitish.* The head and pronotum are scattered with long, bristly black hairs.

Color. Overall uniformly dark yellow-brown to black. The legs are paler than the head, body, and tegmina, often gray to yellow-brown.

Ovipositor. Short, *less than two-thirds* the length of the femur; curves gently upward.

Call. A continuous "riiiiiiiiiiiiiiiiiiiiiiiiiiiiiiiiiiiiiiiiiiiiiiiiiiiiiiiiii." The "i" in "ri" is a soft vowel, as in the word "rigor," a good word to associate with this cricket, as it is one of the first ground crickets to begin calling in spring and one of the last Orthoptera to call it a season in late fall.

Similar Species

    Cuban and Sphagnum Ground Crickets. See accounts on pages 107 and 109 for differences.

Notes. Everyone with a working set of ears has heard this cricket. They are in nearly every patch of lawn (those untreated by chemicals, of course, but even then . . .) in nearly every state in this country. They are a subtle and constant part of the outdoor soundscape, though most people just don't realize they hear them. I find them most noticeable in the fall, when most, if not all of their aural competition has succumbed to the cold. A lone, quivering trill from beneath the fallen leaves allows us to, at least for a moment, put off thoughts of winter.

Illustration on page 110.

Bush Crickets

Subfamily Eneopterinae

Outside of North America, many call katydids bush crickets. The bush crickets in this book, however, are true *crickets* in the family Gryllidae. They're medium in size, somewhat robust, and are found off the ground in trees and shrubs. Unlike the preceding crickets, their hind tibiae have minute teeth on the upper surface between the spines. The second-to-last segment of the tarsus is heart shaped.

The ovipositor is long, somewhat cylindrical, and points upward at a slight angle. Eggs are inserted in plant stems or in crevices between bark.

They feed primarily on deciduous leaves, ferns, flowers, berries, and larger fruit.

There are not a lot of Eneopterinae in the United States, and only two species, representing two genera (*Orocharis* and *Hapithus*) are within our range.

Genus *Orocharis*

While the bush crickets tend to be robust, the *Orocharis* are on the more long and slender side of that scale. Their shape is somewhat like that of a beefy tree cricket. They are primarily nocturnal, as evidenced by the very long antennae, which can be three times the length of the body.

Some of the species have a light and dark color form, both more in cryptic unison with bark than leaf. Their tegmina are long, but the hind wings project beyond them. One of the features that has been used to separate *Orocharis* from our other bush cricket genus, *Hapithus*, is the hearing organ, or *tympanum*, on the front tibiae. In the *Orocharis*, there are two hearing organs—one on the front and one on the back. In the *Hapithus*, there is only one on the back.

The *Orocharis* are far more likely to be heard than seen. They hug the branches of plants, creating a very low profile. Their call is a very rich and loud chirp.

Range. Connecticut and south to Georgia.

Habitat. Deciduous trees and undergrowth. Can often be heard calling from trees and shrubs in urban areas.

Size. $^5/_8$ to $^3/_4$ inch

Description. Slender; *lance shaped*. The head is not as wide as the rear width of the pronotum. Tegmina extend past the tip of the abdomen.

Color. Color is variable. The light form is a mottled uniform pale orange-brown. The dark form is gray with dark mottling. Sides of pronotum have a heavy, dark bar pattern.

Ovipositor. Straight, slender, and projecting up at a slight angle.

Call. A series of short, rich trills. Unlike most of the tree-dwelling Orthoptera, these crickets are better camouflaged on bark than leaves and often call from branches.

Similar Species

    Restless Bush Cricket. The Restless Bush Cricket is more robust; barrel shaped, as opposed to lanceolate. The tegmina fall short of the tip of the abdomen. The tegmina of Jumping Bush Crickets surpass the tip.

    The dorsolateral edges of the tegmina are yellow in the former, not so in Jumping Bush Crickets.

Notes. In preparing this book, I put the word out that I needed a male Jumping Bush Cricket to photograph for the painting reference. I'm fortunate to have a good network of friends who are out in the field a lot. Naturalist Noble Proctor found us our first one. Or I should say it found him! Here's his e-mail to me: "Got back to my car and it was sitting on my dashboard. Quick—roll up the windows. However, it hops down and goes into the air conditioner vent!! I crank up the air conditioner and fan to full—it weathers the storm a bit then pops out."

    When I met him to pick up the insect, he commented on what a jumper it was (it had jumped to the back seat of the car after escaping the vent). I witnessed this myself when I tried to photograph it. They are a well-named species (to *saltate* is to jump)!

Illustration on page 114.

Jumping Bush Cricket

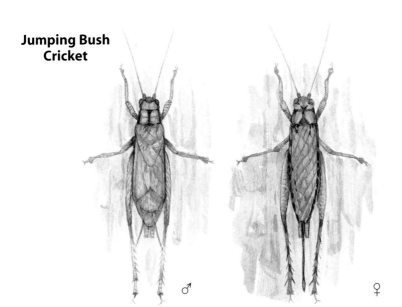

♂   ♀

Restless Bush Cricket

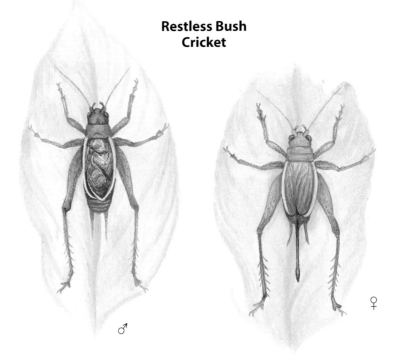

♂   ♀

Genus *Hapithus*

The *Hapithus* are boxy-looking insects, resembling pale, long-legged field crickets. They are largely a South American group, with only three species making it into North America.

Unlike the *Orocharis*, their tegmina do not pass the tip of the abdomen, and the hind wings are either rudimentary, or shorter than the tegmina. The front tibiae possess only one hearing organ, as opposed to the two on *Orocharis*.

In some species, our own *Hapithus agitator* included, the male offers his tegmina as a nuptial meal during mating. The purpose of mate feeding is part of ongoing study, but it is believed that in addition to keeping the female from removing the applied spermatophore, the meal provides nutrients to increase egg production.

It is not uncommon to come across a male with half-eaten stubs for wings. Since the tegmina serve as the calling apparatus, a mated male *Hapithus* will remain silent.

Restless Bush Cricket   *Hapithus agitator*

Range. Connecticut and south to Florida.

Habitat. Found on low plants in damp areas and along weedy roadsides.

Size. ³/₄ to 1 inch

Description. Robust, short, with hind legs appearing long in comparison to its body. The tegmina cover at least three-quarters of the abdomen. In males, the tegmina may be eaten away due to the courtship practice of offering them as a meal to the female during copulation. The second tarsal segments resemble an inflated heart.

Color. Overall pale yellow to reddish brown with dark speckling. Males have a *bold yellow "racing stripe"* along the dorsolateral edges of the tegmina. This stripe occurs in females as well, but tends to be weaker.

Ovipositor. Slender; slightly curved. It approaches the length of the hind femur.

Call. Does not call in our range.

Similar Species

Jumping Bush Cricket. See account on page 113.

Notes. A few years back, I was participating in a Biodiversity Day in the town of Branford, Connecticut. During these events, individuals and teams scour a given area for all manner of flora and fauna within a twenty-four-hour period. I returned from my last foray of the day to the central meeting place. One of the participants, Chris Sullivan, had found an interesting cricket along the edge of a stream. He left it behind for me to identify. What immediately jumped out to me on this cricket were those bright yellow "racing stripes" on the tegmina. This was a new one to me, and when I brought it home to key it out, there was no question it was a Restless Bush Cricket. It turned out to be the first Connecticut, and northernmost, record for this insect, and was yet another example of how little we know about what we have in our own backyards.

I have since come across several others in my travels south and do wonder why they are called "restless." They are actually more on the sluggish end of the scale when it comes to crickets and I would suggest a name change to *Hapithus somniculosus*, Res*ting* Bush Cricket.

Illustration on page 114.

Scaly Crickets

Subfamily Mogoplistinae

Formerly known as the "Wingless Bush Crickets," the Mogoplistinae are small, dorsally flattened, climbing crickets with bodies covered in translucent scales. The females are usually wingless, and the males have very short tegmina. The hind tibiae have no spines, but have small teeth along the upper and lower surface.

This subfamily is represented in this guide by a single species in the genus *Cycloptilum*.

Circle-winged Scaly Crickets—Genus *Cycloptilum*

Also called "Common Scaly Crickets," this is the best represented genus of the Mogoplistinae in the United States. Most, however, are far south of the range covered in this book. While all the references and the specimen data I studied suggest they don't make it as far north as New Jersey, I was able to find a few of them in Ocean County, New Jersey, so include it here.

The *Cycloptilum* are alert little crickets, active among the shrubs, grasses, and within varying levels of trees. The pronotum is very large, growing wider toward the rear. The male tegmina peek out just a short distance from the pronotum (sometimes they are fully concealed) and are absent, or unseen, in the females. Two very long cerci project from the abdomen.

Translucent scales cover the somewhat dorsally flattened body, and the hind femora are relatively short for a cricket.

Despite the reduced tegmina, scaly crickets do call, those calls being high in pitch and ranging from sustained trills to shorter chirps.

Range. New Jersey and south to Florida.

Habitat. Shrubby undergrowth along woods and wetlands, on the leaves and beneath loose bark.

Size. $^1/_4$ to $^3/_8$ inch

Description. Very small and delicate in appearance—similar in overall shape to an earwig. The body has a powdery look, due to the presence of tiny scales that lend this group their name. The cerci in males and females are very long, nearly the length of the body. In males, the wings, tinged with red, extend slightly past the pronotum. In females, the tegmina are greatly reduced. The antennae greatly exceed the length of the body. Tips of the palpi form an *isosceles triangle* (hence the species name of *trigonipalpum*).

Color. Reddish brown; abdomen is considerably darker than the pronotum. Pale scales accentuate the ridges in the abdomen.

Ovipositor. Slightly curved; nearly the length of the abdomen; about half as long as the cerci.

Call. A quiet, buzzy "zeeet-zeeet-zeeet . . . zeeet-zeeeet. . . ." There are several second pauses between each two-to-five-"zeeeet" sequence. Calls at night.

Similar Species. The northern range limit for the other scaly crickets is south of New Jersey. This species can be separated by others in this family by the triangular palpi tips.

Notes. The first time I came upon these insects, it was quite by accident. I was searching some tall grasses outside of Atlantic City along the New Jersey shore, and found them clinging to the stems. I didn't think scaly crickets made it that far north, but there they were. Perhaps they make it even farther north than that. The known ranges of the more cryptic species, which would surely include Forest Scaly Crickets, are described by the relatively few people who have looked for them. With more eyes, and ears, searching for these creatures, there is little doubt we'll find them to be more widespread than what the data currently show.

Forest Scaly Cricket

♂

♀

Tree Crickets

Subfamily Oecanthinae

The tree crickets are slender little insects—slender legs, slender body, and generally pale green to brown. One of the old names for this subfamily is "White Tree Crickets," although only one species, the Snowy Tree Cricket, tends to be pale enough to earn that name. The Oecanthinae inhabit the leaves and flowers of weeds, shrubs, and trees. The Greek translation for the genus *Oecanthus* is "lives in flower." The body is dorsally flattened and they carry their heads horizontally, which is unique for the crickets in our area. Most crickets' heads are vertical to the body. The male tegmina are clear to translucent, lie flat on the body, and are wider than the abdomen. The female tegmina are narrow and wrap around the body.

Males call by lifting their tegmina at about a 45-degree angle from the body, holding them apart to form a wide, translucent heart. They call day and/or night often in the form of a pulsing trill. Lifting the wings at such an angle allows the female to come up from behind and feed on a secretion produced by glands in the upper thorax. She feeds for a considerable length of time before the male ventures to attach his spermatophore from the tip of his abdomen to hers. She continues to feed for some time after this takes place.

Once they uncouple, the female removes the spermatophore and consumes it. It has been theorized that one of the purposes of offering the female a nuptial meal is to distract her long enough to allow the sperm from the spermatophore to inseminate her. It also serves to get her interested in the first place.

Eggs are laid in the bark or pithy stems of herbaceous plants via a drill-like ovipositor.

Tree crickets are predacious, the mainstay of their insect food being aphids. They also eat leaves and fruit.

Smooth-legged Tree Crickets—Genus *Neoxabea*

The *Neoxabea* are separated from the *Oecanthus* by two features. The most obvious is the lack of spines on the upper surface of the hind tibiae. The *Oecanthus* hind tibiae have a few short spines and tiny, sawlike teeth in this region.

Less obvious is the presence of a blunt tooth (*tubercle*) on the basal antenna segment. This is lacking in the *Oecanthus*. The face of the basal antennal segment is unmarked, unlike the basal segment of most of the other tree crickets.

We have just the one species of *Neoxabea*, and fortunately its color and patterning make it easy enough to separate from all the other tree crickets without having to inspect it through a loupe. But have a look anyway. Sometimes it's interesting to see what makes a genus a genus.

Range. Massachusetts and south to Florida.

Habitat. Deciduous treetops; in tangled undergrowth of woodland edges.

Size. $^3/_4$ to 1 inch

Description. Very slender and twiglike in color and shape. Male tegmina are narrow, transparent, and barely wider than the body. The female tegmina are pinkish and have two pairs of long, blackish spots on the upper surface. The spots are often connected by a lateral stripe of dark brown. The head and pronotum range in color from cream to deep red-brown. Legs and antennae are pale yellow.

Antennae Base Markings. The antennae are pale yellow at base with black flecking in the lower quarter of their length. There are no black marks on the basal segments. There is a distinctive, *sharp bump* on the inner, upper surface. That bump is one of the characteristics of the genus *Neoxabea*.

Call. A buzzy, dry trill broken with short pauses. Sometimes the trill is continuous. Sings at night.

Species Similar in Appearance. This is the only species that is overall pale, reddish brown. Note the differences in the members of the tree cricket subfamily in the introduction to this group.

Similar Call

> *Narrow-winged and Davis's Tree Crickets.* See accounts on pages 123 and 130.

Notes. Being an amateur lepidopterist, I often run a blacklight in my yard to attract moths. I can always count on the light luring in a few Two-spotted Tree Crickets throughout the season. Since they're largely arboreal creatures, they would be otherwise difficult to seek out. When I do find them, without the aid of a blacklight, it is usually by chance. They will be in a tangle of grapevines or on the leaves of a sapling at the edge of the woods. They're usually very tame and easy to observe.

Illustration on page 121.

Two-spotted Tree Cricket

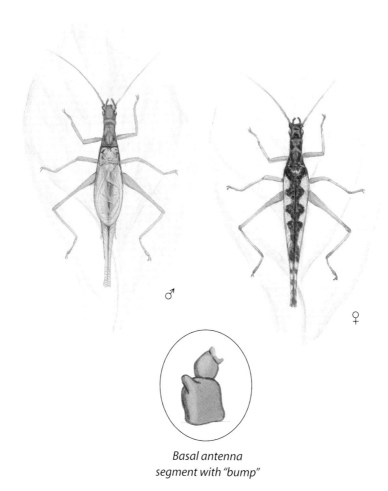

♂

♀

Basal antenna
segment with "bump"

Common Tree Crickets—Genus *Oecanthus*

The *Oecanthus* make up the larger genus of the Oecanthinae and are separated from the *Neoxabea* by the features described in the *Neoxabea* genus account. Their life history is described in the section covering the subfamily.

Identifying Tree Crickets

The most reliable method for telling one *Oecanthus* from the other is by looking at the pattern, or lack thereof, on the face of the basal antennae segments. These would be the first and second segments emanating from the head. The pattern will consist of varying forms and numbers (between zero and four) of black dots and/or dashes. They can be observed by looking head-on at the cricket and, depending upon how sharp your eyesight is, a magnifying lens may be necessary. I've found that by putting the cricket in a clear, flat container, like an empty CD case, you can get a close look at all the features without harming the insect. Use the thicker kind that is made for commercial CDs, as opposed to the slim jewel cases, which may crush them.

The illustrations of the basal segments show the angle at which all of the markings can be seen. Sometimes that just requires a slight rotation from the head-on view. The basal segments of the left antenna appear to the left of the illustrations of the depicted male and female. Bear in mind that there can be a variation on the shapes, and sometimes, number of markings. We have depicted the typical pattern we've observed in the field.

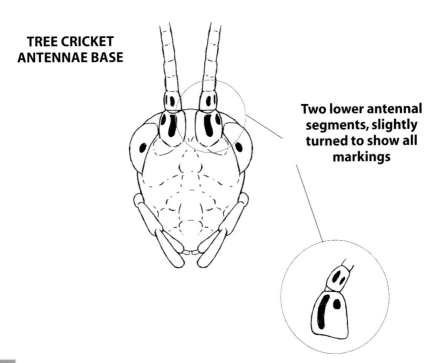

TREE CRICKET ANTENNAE BASE

Two lower antennal segments, slightly turned to show all markings

Narrow-winged Tree Cricket   *Oecanthus niveus*

Range. Vermont and south to Florida.

Habitat. Deciduous trees, high and low; sometimes shrubs and herbaceous plants along edges of fields.

Size. $1/2$ to $5/8$ inch

Description. Slender; pale green. The top of the head in both sexes usually has a diamond-shaped patch ranging in color from *yellow-orange to deep orange.* Sometimes the orange extends into the top of the pronotum and the lower segments of the antennae. The eyes are often powder blue. Tegmina are translucent, with a wash of pale green, and are about one-third as broad at their widest point as long. The legs are often marked with a few small, black spots. The antennae are usually pale yellow-green.

Antennae Base Markings. The bases of the antennae are marked with a bold, black J outlined in white. The second antennal segments contain a slightly curved, oblong dash.

Call. This orange-headed tree cricket produces a soft, pulsing trill, sounding like a ringing phone. The call lasts for about two to six seconds with the pause lasting nearly as long. Calls from late afternoon into the night.

Species Similar in Appearance

Davis's Tree Cricket. This species can also have some orange in the head, but it is usually somewhat washed out and not as rich in color. Note differences in the antennae markings. Those in Davis's form an inverted exclamation point, as opposed to the Narrow-winged's J with a short dash over it.

Snowy Tree Cricket. Both species have orange on top of the head, but it is more prominent in Narrow-winged Tree Crickets. In addition to the difference in antennae markings, the male Snowy Tree Cricket's wings are nearly (but not quite) one-half as broad as long at their widest point. The wings of a male Narrow-winged Tree Cricket are about one-third as broad as long.

Similar Call

Davis's Tree Cricket. While this species also has a pulsing trill, it is noticeably deeper in pitch and the pattern in the length of the trill and silence in between is more irregular.

Two-spotted Tree Cricket. This species also has a pulsing trill, but it is buzzy and "drier," lacking the richness in tone. The pauses in between the calls are considerably shorter, one to several seconds, when compared with the length of the trill. They also call from higher in the trees.

Snowy Tree Cricket. The call of this species is also broken by regular pauses; however, it is a much more rapid call and is more of a "chirp" than trill. The Snowy only calls at night.

Notes. I once had an old cat named Jupiter. She slept a lot in her twilight years. A favorite spot of hers was by a window, outside of which grew a large butterfly bush. One summer evening she began to snore. She never snored before, but I attributed it to her age. Every night, when I'd look over to her by the window, there she was, sleeping, and snoring away. One night, I heard the snoring and looked

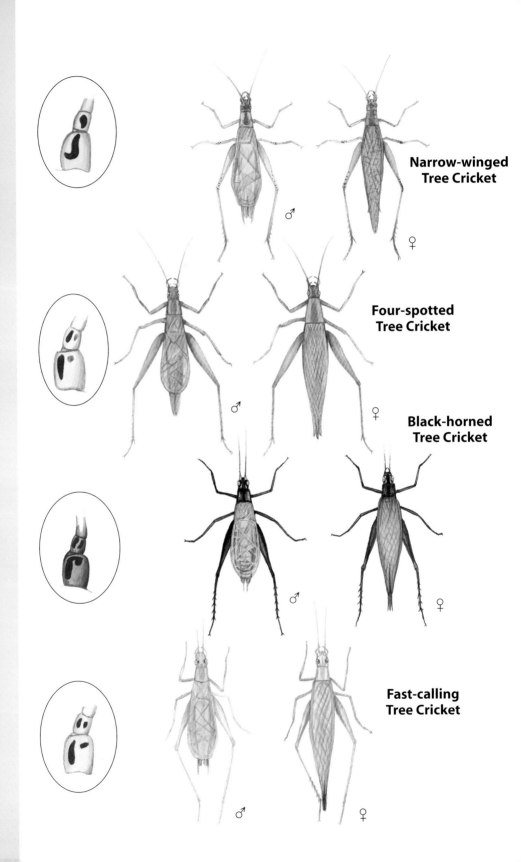

Narrow-winged Tree Cricket

♂ ♀

Four-spotted Tree Cricket

♂ ♀

Black-horned Tree Cricket

♂ ♀

Fast-calling Tree Cricket

♂ ♀

over to the window. She wasn't there. She was at the other end of the room. What I had been hearing was not snoring, but the steady pulse of a Narrow-winged Tree Cricket that had taken up residence in the butterfly bush outside the window.

When I hear these crickets now, I think of my cat Jupiter (who never snored).

Illustration on page 124.

Four-spotted Tree Cricket   *Oecanthus quadripunctatus*

Range. Maine and south to Florida.
Habitat. Fairly low areas; on herbaceous plants in weedy fields and roadsides, and on low branches along edges of woods.
Size. $^1/_2$ to $^5/_8$ inch
Description. The slenderest *Oecanthus* in our range. All parts are uniformly pale green and, except for the antennae bases, are usually without any dark spots or markings. Some individuals, however, will have a few black dots on the hind femora and some will have a pale, orange wash on top of the head. The tegmina are translucent, with a wash of pale green. The antennae are usually somewhat dusky.
Antennae Base Markings. The markings on the base of the antennae vary, but there are *usually four,* hence the name of this cricket. The basal segment usually contains two marks: a bold, black vertical dash toward the inside and a paler rounded spot on the outside. The second segment contains a shorter, yet equally bold, vertical dash on the inside, and a paler, shorter-yet dash on the outside.
Call. A rich, high, continuous trill. Calls day and night.
Species Similar in Appearance
Black-horned Tree Cricket. A light-colored Black-horned Tree Cricket has very similar antennae markings; however, the Four-spotted Tree Cricket lacks the dark shading in the legs, head, and pronotum.
Narrow-winged Tree Cricket. Both share a slender form, but the Narrow-winged Tree Cricket has a narrower head and more spots on the legs. It is best separated, though, by the very different basal antennae patterns.
Fast-calling Tree Cricket. Both insects have four markings on the basal antennae segments; however, those of the Fast-calling Tree Cricket are equally bold and the spot on the outside of the second segment is elongated into a teardrop shape. In the Four-spotted Tree Cricket, the outer marks are paler than the inner marks, and the spot on the outside of the second segment is more rounded and lighter than the mark beside it.
The northern range limit of the Fast-calling Tree Cricket is New Jersey.
Similar Call
Black-horned Tree Cricket. Virtually indistinguishable from the Four-spotted, although the Black-horned does seem to call a bit more loudly.
Pine Tree Cricket. The trill is very similar in pitch, but Pine Tree Crickets call primarily from high in conifers.
Fast-calling Tree Cricket. While the trill is produced with more rapid pulses than the other tree crickets, it is difficult to separate this species from Four-spotted and

Black-horned Tree Crickets solely by ear. If the insect is calling north of New Jersey, however, you can most likely rule out the Fast-calling Tree Cricket.

Notes. I tend to find these crickets in the very same habitat as Black-horned Tree Crickets, but rarely do I find both in the same place. They inhabit upland fields abounding in goldenrod, bush clover, aster, yarrow, and Queen Ann's Lace. As with the closely related Black-horned Tree Cricket, they begin to trill in the middle of the afternoon and are easy to find among the weeds.

Illustration on page 124.

Black-horned Tree Cricket   *Oecanthus nigricornis*

Range. Maine and south to western North Carolina.

Habitat. Fairly low areas; on herbaceous plants in weedy fields and roadsides, and on low branches along edges of woods.

Size. $^1/_2$ to $^3/_4$ inch

Description. Head, pronotum, legs, antennae, and cerci are brownish black. Tegmina are yellow-green. The abdomen, which can be seen through the translucent wings, is yellow-green, with brownish black along the segments. Bear in mind that there are paler forms of this insect, but the *legs and antennae will still be dark.*

Antennae Base Markings. In the more frequently encountered black form, the black bases of the antennae obscure the markings. In lighter forms, the markings on the base of the antennae vary, but there are usually four. The basal segment will contain two marks: a bold, black vertical dash toward the inside and a bold tear-shaped spot on the outside. They sometimes bleed into each other. The second segment contains a shorter, yet equally bold, vertical dash on the inside, and shorter-yet, bold dash on the outside.

Call. A rich, high, continuous trill. Calls day and night.

Species Similar in Appearance

Four-spotted Tree Cricket. See account on page 125 and above.

Pine Tree Cricket. Both species can have dark antennae, and while head, pronotum, and legs of Pine Tree Crickets are darker than the wings and body, they are yellow-brown to reddish brown, not black. The tegmina are also deep "pine needle green," as opposed to Black-horned Tree Crickets' pale, yellowish tegmina. See account on page 128 for differences in basal antennae markings.

Pine Tree Crickets inhabit conifers, not open fields and herbaceous edges.

Similar Call

Four-spotted Tree Cricket. See account on page 125.

Pine Tree Cricket. The trill is very similar in pitch, but Pine Tree Crickets call primarily from high in conifers.

Fast-calling Tree Cricket. While the trill is produced with more rapid pulses than that of the other tree crickets, it is difficult to separate this species from Four-spotted and Black-horned Tree Crickets solely by ear. If the insect is calling north of New Jersey, however, you can most likely rule out the Fast-calling Tree Cricket.

Notes. Black-horned Tree Crickets are probably the most accessible species in this group. They are especially easy to find on goldenrod flowers late in the season. They call on sunny afternoons and are not very shy about being watched.

Illustration on page 124.

Fast-calling Tree Cricket   *Oecanthus celerinictus*

Range. New Jersey and south to Florida.

Habitat. Weedy fields and roadsides, areas with low vegetation.

Size. $1/2$ to $5/8$ inch

Description. Males have rather slender, nearly transparent tegmina. The head, pronotum, body, and legs are pale yellow-green. A short, thin, brown "eyebrow" often hugs the top of the eye. The antennae are lighter at the base and grow darker, from pale gray to black, toward the tip. Sparse flecking can be present in the hind legs and tegmina.

Antennae Base Markings. The basal antenna segment has a heavy, lateral dash toward the inside. A heavy, *teardrop-shaped* spot shares that segment toward the outside. The second segment has two parallel dashes shorter than the dash below, the inside mark usually a little longer than the outside mark.

Call. A continuous, high, rapid trill, sometimes interrupted by a brief pause. Calls day and night.

Species Similar in Appearance

Four-spotted Tree Cricket. See account on pages 125 and 126.

Similar Call

Four-spotted and Black-horned Tree Crickets. While the trill of the Fast-calling Tree Cricket is produced with more rapid pulses than the other tree crickets, it is difficult to separate this species from Four-spotted and Black-horned Tree Crickets solely by ear. If the insect is calling north of New Jersey, however, you can most likely rule out the Fast-calling Tree Cricket.

Pine Tree Cricket. Pine Tree Crickets call from conifers while Fast-calling Tree Crickets call from lower, broadleaf and herbaceous vegetation. The trill is also higher in pitch that that of the Pine Tree Cricket. If the insect you hear is calling north of New Jersey, you can most likely rule out the Fast-calling Tree Cricket.

Notes. *Celer*, the Latin root of the name *Celerinictus*, means "swift." This refers to the frequency of the pulses produced by the stridulating tegmina—more are given per second. In sonograms of the call, individual pulses that form the trill are closer together than those produced by the other tree crickets. It is possible to notice the rapidity of the trill when compared with that of other species, but the difference to the ear can be subtle. The faster pulsing does tend to give it a higher pitch.

Illustration on page 124.

Range. Maine and south to Florida.

Habitat. Upper branches of conifers (pine, hemlock, fir, cedar, larch); sometimes found in the lower branches and understory.

Size. ⁵/₈ to ³/₄ inch

Description. Our most attractive tree cricket. Head and pronotum orange-brown to reddish brown (the color of the base of pine needles) with a dark stripe running dorsally from the face and nearly to the end of the pronotum. The legs are also reddish brown, but the hind femur can be green. The wings are translucent and *deep green,* like the pine needles the insect is usually found on. The antennae are reddish brown to black; however, the basal segments are pale yellow-brown.

Antennae Base Markings. The base segment is pale yellow-brown with a long black dash on the inner edge and slanted spot near the top of the outer edge. The second segment has two parallel dashes, the outer dash just a little shorter than the inner dash.

Call. A rich, high, continuous trill. Calls day and night.

Species Similar in Appearance

    Black-horned Tree Cricket. See account on page 126.

Similar Call

    Four-spotted, Black-horned, and Fast-calling Tree Crickets. See accounts on pages 125, 126, and 127.

Notes. These crickets are so similar in appearance to the pines they inhabit, they are nearly impossible to find by just "looking." One singing, eye-level, Pine Tree Cricket gave the author and illustrator of this book a run for the money for about half an hour. We circled and circled the pine, searching every branch and needle—it never sounded less than inches away! We finally found it, wings in the air, in a little fork in the trunk.

    What works best is sweeping the calling area with a net—and a bit of patience. But of all the tree crickets, this is the one you really want to see. They're as much a treat for the eyes as they are the ears.

Illustration on page 129.

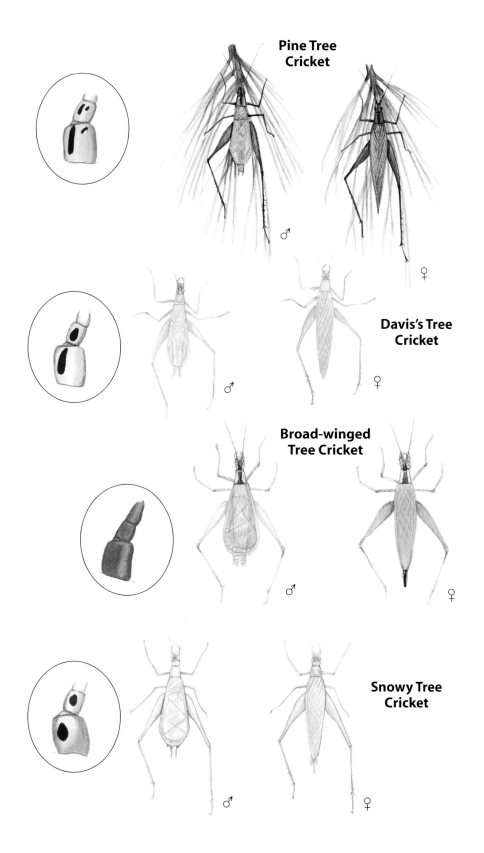

Pine Tree Cricket

♂　　♀

Davis's Tree Cricket

♂　　♀

Broad-winged Tree Cricket

♂　　♀

Snowy Tree Cricket

♂　　♀

Range. Vermont and south to Florida.

Habitat. High and low in deciduous trees, most notably, dogwoods; sometimes in shrubs and herbaceous plants along edges of fields.

Size. $^5/_8$ to $^3/_4$ inch

Description. A fairly slender insect; very pale, ranging from buffy to whitish green. The legs and antennae are also pale and somewhat translucent. The tegmina are pale, whitish green. Some individuals may have a very light wash of orange on top of the head.

Antennae Base Markings. A black, elongated dash is present on the face of the basal antenna segment. A slightly elongated dot is directly above it on the second segment. Together they form the *inverted exclamation point,* which gives this species its scientific name.

Call. A rich, high trill of uneven lengths, broken by uneven pauses. Calls day and night.

Species Similar in Appearance

Narrow-winged Tree Cricket. See account on page 125.

Similar Call

Narrow-winged Tree Cricket. See account on page 125.

Two-spotted Tree Cricket. This species also has a pulsing trill, but it is buzzy and "drier," lacking the richness in tone.

Snowy Tree Cricket. The call of this species is also broken by pauses; it is a much more rapid and steady call, however, and is more of a "chirp" than a trill.

Notes. Instead of assigning this tree cricket with a common name to match its scientific name (Exclamation Mark Tree Cricket), it was named for William T. Davis (1862–1945), a self-taught naturalist who lived in Staten Island, New York, where he first discovered this species.

In Staten Island you can go to the William T. Davis National Wildlife Refuge, the first wildlife sanctuary created in New York.

Be sure to listen for Mr. Davis's crickets in the trees.

Illustration on page 129.

Broad-winged Tree Cricket — *Oecanthus latipennis*

Range. Connecticut and south to Florida.

Habitat. Lower vegetation; shrubs and herbaceous plants in fields and along woodland edges.

Size. $^5/_8$ to $^7/_8$ inch

Description. Males have very broad wings (which give them their name), about half as broad at their widest point as long; head, body, and legs range from creamy white to pale whitish green. The pronotum often has a broad, green lateral stripe on the upper face. Top of the head is a deep *raspberry color,* which spreads into the lower segments of the antennae.

Antennae Base Markings. This species lacks the black antennae markings present in the others. They are instead infused with *deep red.*

Call. A very loud, rich, continuous trill. Sings late afternoon into the night.

Species Similar in Appearance. This is the only species with deep red on top of the head and into the lower portion of the antennae.

Similar Call

Four-spotted, Black-horned, and Fast-calling Tree Crickets. These crickets also have a continuous trill and call from lower vegetation. The Broad-winged Tree Cricket trill, however, is considerably louder, richer in tone, and deeper in pitch.

Notes. This is the loudest-calling tree cricket. One cannot ignore the fact that the loudest cricket just happens to have a song-producing apparatus (tegmina) with the greatest surface area. It is fortunate for those of us who have these crickets in our yard that their song is pleasing to the ear.

Illustration on page 129.

Range. Maine and south to Georgia. Mostly absent from the middle to southern coast.

Habitat. Lower vegetation; shrubs and herbaceous plants in fields and along woodland edges. Also at various levels in deciduous trees.

Size. ⁵/₈ to ³/₄ inch

Description. Males have broad wings, nearly half as broad as long at their widest point. The head, pronotum, abdomen, and legs are *ivory white to pale green.* Wings are nearly transparent, but often tinged with pale green. The top of the head is washed in pale yellow to orange. The antennae are ivory white to pale green.

Antennae Base Markings. The basal antenna segment has a heavy black round dot toward the inside. The second segment has a heavy, black oval dot in the middle.

Call. A series of loud rich, evenly spaced chirps; faster and higher in pitch on warm nights; slower and lower in pitch on colder nights. Sings at night.

Species Similar in Appearance

> *Narrow-winged Tree Cricket.* See account on page 123.

Similar Call

> *Narrow-winged and Davis's Tree Crickets.* See accounts on pages 123 and 130.

Notes. There was confusion some time ago over which was the real "Snowy Tree Cricket." For over a century, the species was called *niveus*, which is the current species name for the Narrow-winged Tree Cricket (which was then *angustipennis*). The taxonomists settled on naming it after Bentley B. Fulton, who in 1915 wrote the orthopteral masterpiece *The Tree Crickets of New York: Life History and Bionomics.*

Also known as the "Thermometer Cricket," this is the species long used to estimate the outdoor temperature. If you add forty to the number of chirps in thirteen seconds, the sum is within a few degrees of the temperature in Fahrenheit.

Illustration on page 129.

Trigs/Sword-bearing Crickets

Subfamily Trigonidiinae

*T*rigs are very small crickets, rarely over a half-inch long, that live in grasses, sedges, shrubs, and the tops of trees. They go by many names—bush cricket, sword-bearing cricket, sword-tailed cricket, winged bush cricket, and trig. I tend to use that last one, which is just a shortened form of the subfamily name. The Trigonidiinae are placed in this group by virtue of their laterally flattened, saber-shaped ovipositors.

They are also unique in having three pairs of long spurs on the hind tibiae. The Nemobiinae (ground crickets), which can look similar to some of the trig genera, have more than three. This group shares with the Eneopterinae (bush crickets) a bilobed second tarsal segment, but in the trigs, it is hairy beneath. They are also considerably smaller than the members of that subfamily.

The tegmina are usually fully developed and are lifted at about a 45-degree angle when stridulating. They produce high, tinkling or scratchy calls.

Trigs feed on a wide range of food including leaves, flowers, insect eggs, and small insects.

Leaf-mouthed Trigs—Genus *Phyllopalpus*

The *Phyllopalpus* are a small group, with all but one of the members south of the United States. The name refers to the last segment of the maxillary palpi, which is paddle or leaf shaped. They were formerly in the genus *Phylloscyrtus*, meaning "curved leaf." This could have referred to the oval palpi, but it also fits with the unique, convex, beetlelike tegmina of the female.

Range. New Jersey and south to Florida.

Habitat. Lower vegetation surrounding wetlands.

Size. $^3/_{16}$ to $^5/_{16}$ inch

Description. A very attractive, or "handsome," insect. The head and pronotum is a *deep cherry red*. The tegmina, abdomen, and palpi (which are very large) range from deep purple to black. The hind wings are always concealed. Legs are pale greenish yellow and the antennae are multitoned; black at the base, then white toward the lower quarter, then black again to the tip. The tegmina in females are *convex,* giving the cricket a beetlelike appearance.

Ovipositor. Dark brown to black; strongly curved and more than half the length of the hind femur.

Call. A high, rapid, "skritchy," irregular trill of short pulses. Calls day and night.

Species Similar in Appearance. No other cricket in our range has the coloration of this species.

Similar Call

Round-tipped Conehead. While the songs of both species have somewhat of a high, buzzy, "live wire" quality, the call of the Round-tipped Conehead is smoother, more continuous, as opposed to the stuttery call of the Handsome Trig.

Notes. Philip Uhler, being a librarian (and entomologist), had many words at his disposal when choosing a name for this species in 1864. He went with *pulchellus,* which means "pretty or beautiful."

While the tropics are filled with brightly colored Gryllidae, this is the one we get, and it is well named.

Illustration on page 135.

Handsome Trig

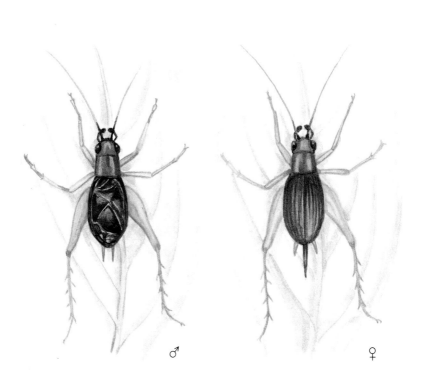

♂ ♀

Sword-tailed Crickets—Genus *Anaxipha*

This is a fairly large genus containing about 127 species worldwide. They are small, pale straw to brown (never green), and can be separated from the *Phyllopalpus* by their less-rounded, more strongly triangular terminal palpi. With only one *Phyllopalpus* and one *Anaxipha* to deal with in our area, however, one need not make that distinction, as they are very different in appearance.

The females bear a long, upward-curving ovipositor, hence the Greek-based genus name *Anaxipha*, meaning "upraised sword."

Say's Trig

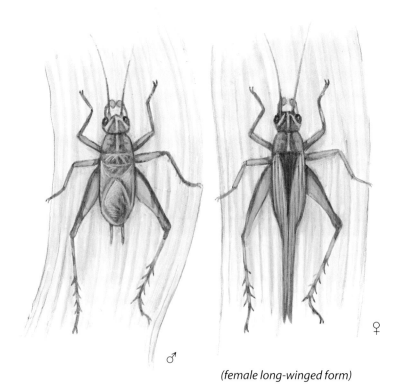

♂

♀

(female long-winged form)

Range. Connecticut and south to Florida.

Habitat. Lower vegetation; grasses, sedges, shrubs, and herbaceous plants along the edges of wetlands. Also in upland areas, in the lower vegetation. Unlike the ground crickets this species resembles, they are usually *on* the stems, branches, and leaves of plants, as opposed to on the ground beneath them.

Size. $^3/_{16}$ to $^1/_4$ inch

Description. Very small and delicate-appearing. Overall pale yellow-brown to reddish brown, with a dark, nearly black, abdomen. The face has *three brown stripes:* two emanate from the bottom of each eye and join at the lower face; one runs down the center of the face. The legs are pale straw, with the hind femur possessing a thin, dark brown stripe along the bottom edge. In the short-winged form, the tegmina are translucent with a yellowish tinge, nearly reaching the tip of the abdomen in the male, and covering about three-fifths to seven-eighths of the abdomen in females. In the long-winged form, the tegmina and hind wings have a pinkish hue, the hind wings extending far beyond the tip of the abdomen. The antennae range from pale yellow to brown-black.

Ovipositor. Black; strongly curved and about half the length of the hind femur. The genus name of *Anaxipha* compares the shape and position of the ovipositor to an upraised sword.

Call. A high, sustained, "breathy" trill. Calls day and night.

Species Similar in Appearance

Columbian Trig. While this species shares the same overall shape, its pale yellow-green coloration immediately separates it from the Say's Trig. It is also more likely to be up in trees, as opposed to in the lower vegetation.

Ground Crickets. A quick look at the size and shape of a Say's Trig may suggest a ground cricket; unlike ground crickets, however, trigs climb plants. See also the descriptions on pages 98 and 133 for each subfamily.

Similar Call

Carolina Ground Cricket. Both have a continuous trill, but the trill of the Say's Trig is less buzzy.

Sphagnum Ground Cricket. Both have a somewhat breathy, high trill, but Sphagnum Ground Crickets break their trills into approximately ten-second sessions, and are confined to open sphagnum bogs. Say's Trig calls are continuous and, while they may be found along the bog's edge, they are not likely to be in the sphagnum.

Cuban Ground Cricket. The trill of this species is buzzier, less "breathy."

Notes. Years ago, while net-sweeping the grasses along the Connecticut River, I picked up what I thought was an interesting ground cricket. I put it in a glass jar, where it proceeded to climb, like a little spider, up the edge. No ground cricket does that! I couldn't wait to get home to figure out what this actually was. It turned out to be my first *Anaxipha exigua.* I had to be extra mindful of the size of the holes in the top of the container for this one.

Illustration on page 136.

Some time later, while researching this species further, I came across a paper authored in 1956 by Bentley Fulton (who has a tree cricket named for him). He wrote, "Unlike true ground crickets, such as *Nemobius*, they are able to walk up the side of a glass jar."

I've often had the conversation with other naturalists about the satisfaction in reading later an account of a unique behavior you'd witnessed in the field. I wonder how many others, upon catching this cricket for the first time, said, "Hey, it's crawling up the side of the jar!"

Sword-tailed Trigs—Genus *Cyrtoxipha*

Cyrtoxipha, meaning "curved sword," is a small genus, with one species making it, barely, into the range covered in this book. They share the triangular palpi with the *Anaxipha*, as well as the upcurved, saber-shaped ovipositor. They are most easily separated from them, however, by their green color. The *Anaxipha* are always some shade of brown. If you are color-blind, there is another way to distinguish the two. The *interocular* area (between the inner, midpoint of the eyes) of *Anaxipha* is rounded. That same area is flat in *Cyrtoxipha*.

There are many other differences between the two species we have in our area, which are highlighted in their descriptions.

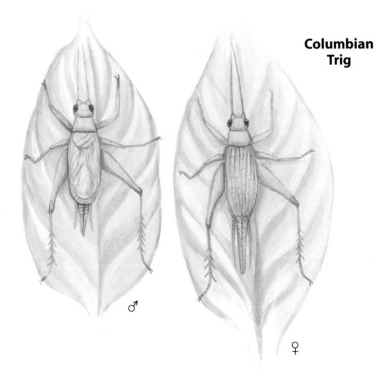

Columbian Trig

♂

♀

Range. Southern New Jersey and south to Florida.

Habitat. Varying levels, but often upper, in deciduous trees in natural areas, as well as suburban and urban neighborhoods.

Size. ¹/₄ to ¹/₃ inch

Description. Very small and delicate in appearance. Overall *pale yellow-green*. Eyes are yellow to red, and are a different color from the head. The tegmina are translucent and have a yellow-green tinge, often with a bit of deep orange, the result of the color of the abdomen showing through. They range between covering about seven-eighths of the abdomen, to exceeding its length. The hind wings are long and extend well beyond the tegmina. The antennae are paler at the base, growing darker toward the tips. The tips of the spines arming the hind tibia are often black.

Ovipositor. Strongly curved and about three-fifths the length of the hind femur; black. The genus *Cyrtoxipha* makes reference to the ovipositor, meaning "curved sword."

Call. A series of high, steady, short, tinkling trills; spaces between trills are about equal to the length of the trill. They are often synchronized with the trills of other males.

Species Similar in Appearance

Say's Trig. See account on page 137.

Tree Crickets. Most tree crickets are similar in color, and many share the same habitat as the Columbian Trig; however, no tree cricket has hind wings a third longer than the tegmina. In addition to other morphological differences, a tree cricket's head is more long than wide. A Columbian Trig's head is more wide than long.

Similar Call

Snowy Tree Cricket. Both species produce a steady series of trills, but the "chirp" of a Snowy Tree Cricket is lower in pitch and of a richer quality: "chir-chir-chir. . . ." The short "trills" of a Columbian Trig are considerably higher, sounding like "tzee-tzee-tzee. . . ."

Tinkling Ground Cricket. The "tink-tink-tink . . ." of Tinkling Ground Crickets sounds similar, but can easily be ruled out by their habitat. They always call from the ground, whereas the Columbian Trigs call from the trees. The call of the former is also more mechanical than the pulsing call of the trigs.

Notes. I flew down to Georgia to rent a car and drive north up the coast back to Connecticut. My reason for doing this was to hunt for crickets and katydids. I spent my first couple nights in Savannah, where, as I drove through the neighborhoods, I was treated to the chorusing of Columbian Trigs in the moss-laden oaks. Those trigs were with me in every state as I traveled north, in the trees in the busiest developments and the quietest sanctuaries. I finally bid them farewell in Ocean County, New Jersey.

Illustration on page 138.

AUTHOR'S NOTE

I make my living as a writer and illustrator, not an entomologist. There, you have my confession. What, you may ask, gives me the audacity to write a field guide on insects? Well, when I started out on this project, there were no guides to katydids or crickets to my area—nothing in print at least. Closest to fitting the bill was a largely technical book on Canadian Orthoptera, which is a great piece of work, but more for those already committed fairly deeply to the subject.

My thought was that I knew more than most people about these insects, and what I didn't know, I could learn. Little did I know how much work this would involve; I discuss more of my "training" in the introductory sections of the book.

What I also didn't know was that at about the time I was hatching this idea, there were others hatching similar ideas. A couple of them beat me to the punch. While it would have been nice to be the first to put out a guide to this group for the general public, I guess we took too long to put this book together.

Interest breeds interest, though. And I am happy that Capinera, Scott, and Walker with their guide (*Field Guide to Grasshoppers, Katydids, and Crickets of the United States*) and Elliot and Hershberger with theirs (*The Songs of Insects*) have whet the appetites for this once underrepresented family. Yes, I winced when I saw how good their books are. But I also felt some relief that we are covering different areas, a good number of different species, and approached our books very differently in how we chose to depict our subjects (for example, we chose to show all of the females in addition to the males).

When I first had the idea to do this guide, I knew right away that I would not be the one painting the plates. While the line drawings are mine, my painting style is not right for this job. I also knew from the first spark of the idea whom I wanted as the artist. Mike DiGiorgio, a friend of mine who lives just one town away, is a wildlife artist. He mostly does bird paintings and has contributed to a number of avian field guides. I remember seeing a couple of insect drawings he did for some newspaper articles. They were just quick line drawings, but something about them made them stand out from insect drawings done by other illustrators. Mike's bugs had *weight*. They looked as if they were affected by the laws of gravity. They looked alive on the page, and these were just line drawings! I wanted him to do the book.

Mike also made recordings. His Marantz recorder had documented the sounds of numerous birds and amphibians. Some were used in books, and he did all the sound engineering on his own. The fact that I was thinking it would be nice to have a CD accompany the book made his signing on for this even more attractive. But, would a bird artist be interested in doing paintings of katydids?

I'll never forget my phone call to him: "Hey Mike, what do you think about crickets and katydids?" I asked.

"I was just out recording them in my yard last night," he answered.

It was meant to be.

We realized early on, though, that Mike could not be the one solely responsible for making the recordings. While we were together in the field many times, most of the field research was my job. It made no sense to send me out among the bugs and pass on the opportunities to record them. So I bought a Marantz recorder and a shotgun microphone. The recorder stores the data on a flash card, the kind used in digital cameras. It's a great piece of technology as there are no moving parts to get jammed up. I found myself surprised to learn that the thrill of catching a good call was as exhilarating as actually seeing the insect!

It took us eight years to do this book; eight years of feeding hungry crickets and katydids in our studios; eight years of hunting down calls; eight years of amassing live photos of males and females; eight years of visiting museums. There were times I would come home in the wee hours of the morning, after hours of listening to chorus after chorus of insects, and I'd still hear them. I'm not kidding. Their phantom songs would continue to call in my ears as my head hit the pillow.

This was truly a collaborative effort, and my first. All of my books prior have been solo projects, and I have to say it was nice to share the experience for a change. In the end, we got to know seventy-four species of katydids and crickets. They're all in this book.

—J. H.

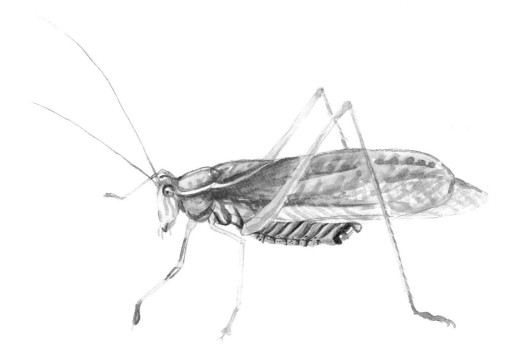

AUDIO GUIDE

1. **Introduction**
2. **Slender Meadow Katydid** *Conocephalus fasciatus*
   The call consists of a series of soft, locomotive-like ticks, followed by a sustained, sputtery trill.
3. **Short-winged Meadow Katydid** *Conocephalus brevipennis*
   Listen for one to five soft, liquid, "tsicks," followed by a brief, soft, buzzy trill.
4. **Saltmarsh Meadow Katydid** *Conocephalus spartinae*
   The call is a very soft, high, sustained, rapid-sputtering buzz, sometimes preceded by short "tsicks." A slight breeze rustling the grass can be enough to mask the sound to the human ear.
5. **Black-sided Meadow Katydid** *Conocephalus nigropleurum*
   Listen for long phrases of buzzy whirs blended with rapid ticking.
6. **Straight-lanced Meadow Katydid** *Conocephalus strictus*
   The call is a soft, buzzy, continuous whir coming from upland and dry grassy areas.
7. **Woodland Meadow Katydid** *Conocephalus nemoralis*
   The song consists of short, gentle buzzes, given steadily, but with varying spaces between. It will also tick either independently, or prior to its call.
8. **Red-headed Meadow Katydid** *Orchelimum erythrocephalum*
   Listen for a sharp, wet "tsick," followed by a buzzy burr. This is repeated continually in rapid sequence. As with most of the *Orchelimum*, they will sometimes just "tick."
9. **Handsome Meadow Katydid** *Orchelimum pulchellum*
   The call consists of a couple quick "tsicks," or a short series of them, followed by a more sustained, buzzy trill. As with most of the *Orchelimum*, they will sometimes just "tick."
10. **Black-legged Meadow Katydid** *Orchelimum nigripes*
    Its call consists of a couple quick ticks, or a short series of them, followed by a more sustained, buzzy trill. As with most of the *Orchelimum*, they will sometimes just "tick."
11. **Common Meadow Katydid** *Orchelimum vulgare*
    Listen for a sustained buzz that grows louder toward the end. Sometimes the buzz is accompanied by a long series of "tsicks."
12. **Gladiator Meadow Katydid** *Orchelimum gladiator*
    Gladiators give several "tsicks," followed by a sustained, soft whir that grows louder toward the end. They will often forgo the sustained whir and just "tick."
13. **Lesser Pine Katydid** *Orchelimum minor*
    Their call is a series of short, bubbly sputters.
14. **Seaside Meadow Katydid** *Orchelimum fidicinium*
    Note the short, fluttery, buzzy sequences. The first set of calls was recorded in the studio. It is followed by several individuals calling in a salt marsh.

15. **Round-tipped Conehead** *Neoconocephalus retusus*
    Its steady, high-pitched, "live wire" buzz can be heard from late afternoon and into the night.
16. **Robust Conehead** *Neoconocephalus robustus*
    The call is a very loud, continuous buzz. In 1874, the entomologist Samuel Scudder compared it to the call of the Dog-day Cicada.
17. **Broad-tipped Conehead** *Neoconocephalus triops*
    Listen for a steady buzz that seems to "trip over itself." The stridulation is broken at regular intervals of one to two seconds. This is the only conehead with a call broken in this manner.
18. **Caudell's Conehead** *Neoconocephalus caudellianus*
    Listen for a loud, slow, steady and buzzy "dzeeet . . . dzeeet . . . dzeeet. . . ." The Long-beaked Conehead has a similar steady call, but there is a more lisping quality to it.
19. **Eastern Swordbearer** *Neoconocephalus ensiger*
    The call of this common species consists of a series of rapid, lisping buzzes. It brings to mind the sound of a fast-moving train.
20. **Long-beaked or Slightly Musical Conehead** *Neoconocephalus exiliscanorus*
    The call is a steady series of lispy "ziits." It is a softer sound than the harsh call of the Nebraska Conehead, which is absent from the coast.
21. **Nebraska Conehead** *Neoconocephalus nebrascensis*
    Unlike many of the species in this group, the call can be given in the middle of the day. It consists of a steady series of high, loud buzzes, each with a second or two pause in between. There's a somewhat angry quality to it. The Slightly Musical Conehead has a similar, steady call, but with a more lispy sound.
22. **Black-nosed Conehead** *Neoconocephalus melanorhinus*
    The call is a continuous, high-pitched electric buzz. It is similar to that of the Round-tipped Conehead, but unlike the Black-nosed Conehead, the Round-tipped Conehead is not restricted to tidal flats.
23. **Marsh Conehead** *Neoconocephalus palustris*
    Listen for a sustained, somewhat weak, high-pitched "zeeeeeeeeeeee. . . ." It is a little higher in pitch than the similar sounding call of the Round-tipped Conehead.
24. **Cattail Conehead** *Bucrates malivolans*
    Listen for a steady, questioning, "tchir-tchir-tchir . . . ?"
25. **Oblong-winged Katydid** *Amblycorypha oblongifolia*
    The call is a short, harsh "ski-di-dit!" or "skritch-it" given at irregular intervals.
26. **Carinate Katydid** *Amblycorypha carinata*
    The call is a high, somewhat harsh, lisping "zit," or "zi-deet," often repeated regularly with a few seconds in between.
27. **Rattler Round-winged Katydid** *Amblycorypha rotundifolia*
    The call is a high, sputtering rattle. It often gives a few introductory sputters, sounding like someone trying to start a tiny flooded two-cycle engine. Then it gives a more sustained sputter, lasting several seconds.

28. Clicker Round-winged Katydid *Amblycorypha alexanderi*

A steady series of high "zits."

29. Lesser Angle-wing *Microcentrum retinerve*

It produces a rapid, lispy rattle, like a rushed version of the Common True Katydid's call, which is often heard in the background while this insect is calling.

30. Greater Angle-wing *Microcentrum rhombifolium*

This species has two calls. One is an uneven, rapid series of ticks, sounding like two pebbles being tapped together. The other call is a lisping "tzip," which may be repeated a number of times.

31. Northern Bush Katydid *Scudderia septentrionalis*

The call consists of a series of wet ticks followed by a rapid succession of "dzee-dzee-dzee-dzee. . . ."

32. Fork-tailed Bush Katydid *Scudderia furcata*

Listen for a wet, isolated "tzip," sometimes given in a sequence with several seconds in between. Note that the Treetop Bush Katydid has a similar call, but they tend to call from the tops of coniferous trees. The Greater Angle-wing also has a "zip" call, but they, too, would be in the tops of trees.

33. Treetop Bush Katydid *Scudderia fasciata*

The call consists of a single "tsip" repeated at irregular intervals; sometimes fairly close together, sometimes minutes apart. The call is nearly identical to that of the Fork-tailed Bush Katydid; the Treetop Katydid, however, usually calls from the tops of trees (most frequently conifers). While Fork-taileds can also call from trees, they tend to be in the understory.

34. Curve-tailed Bush Katydid *Scudderia curvicauda*

The sound is similar to that of the Fork-tailed Bush Katydid; however, the "zips" are slightly less lispy and are given in a sequence of three: "zip-zip-zip . . . zip-zip-zip. . . ." There will often be another "zip" or two added to the sequence.

35. Texas Bush Katydid *Scudderia texensis*

Note the three very different calls of this katydid. One sounds like a very sped up, but quieter, version of a True Katydid and is given at night. The individual notes (three or four), merge to sound something like "zi-di-dit." The dusk call consists of a series of wet "ticks" and the day call is a varying train of rapid "zits." The female also gives a quiet, lispy tick.

36. Broad-winged Bush Katydid *Scudderia pistillata*

One call begins with a lispy, rapid-sequence "zick-zick-zick." After a pause it adds a slightly louder note or two: "zick-zick-zick-ZICK ZICK." Then another pause and another couple notes are added, those notes louder yet: "zick-zick-zick-zick-zick-ZICK ZICK." It will do this a handful of times before starting over. It also gives a series of crackling, wet "ticks" and a very short, rapid, buzzy "zi-di-dip."

37. Common True Katydid *Pterophylla camellifolia*

The call is a very loud and repeated, "Tch-tch-tch . . . tch-tch-tch . . . ," which was interpreted as, "kay-ty-did . . . kay-ty-did. . . ." Often an extra note or two will be added, especially farther south in their range. True katydids synchronize their calls, dominating the sounds of the summer nights. The call gets deeper, raspier, and slower as the temperature cools.

38. **Protean Shieldback** *Atlanticus testaceus*
Listen for a lazy series of high, sputtery buzzes coming from low along the edges of woodland trails and borders of thickets. The calls vary in length and can be broken with irregular intervals of silence.

39. **American Shieldback** *Atlanticus americanus*
It produces a lazy, but steady, series of high sputtery buzzes.

40. **Roesel's Katydid** *Metrioptera roeselii*
The call is a sputtering buzz lasting a couple seconds and given at regular intervals. It can also produce a more sustained buzz.

41. **Northern Mole Cricket** *Neocurtilla hexadactyla*
The Northern Mole Cricket tells you where it lives, producing a burry "dirt-dirt-dirt . . ." from the mouth of its underground burrow.

42. **Fall Field Cricket** *Gryllus pennsylvanicus*
The calls of the Fall and Spring Field cricket are virtually indistinguishable. They are best separated by the time of year the adults are calling. The Spring Field Crickets reach maturity April through July. The Fall Field Crickets occur as adults from August through the first few frosts. There can be an overlap of the two species from late July to early August.
      Listen for the familiar rich, and loud, "chirp . . . chirp . . . chirp. . . ."

43. **Spring Field Cricket** *Gryllus veletis*
As mentioned in the prior track, Spring and Fall Field Crickets are best separated by the time of year in which the adults call. Spring Field Crickets call April through July. Fall Field Crickets call from August through the first few frosts.
      Listen for the familiar rich, and loud, "chirp . . . chirp . . . chirp. . . ."

44. **Sand Field Cricket** *Gryllus firmus*
The call is a rich "churp . . . churp . . . churp," similar to that of the Fall and Spring Field Crickets, but a little deeper in pitch.

45. **Eastern Striped Cricket** *Miogryllus saussurei*
The call is a slow "zeet?" given at intervals of several seconds.

46. **House Cricket** *Acheta domesticus*
Listen for the high, rich, and burry "cheerp . . . cheerp . . . cheerp. . . ."

47. **Japanese Burrowing Cricket** *Velarifictorus micado*
The song consists of a series of burry chirps: "cheer-cheer-cheer . . . ," strung closely together. It is similar to that of the *Gryllus* species, but the call is more rapid.

48. **Spotted Ground Cricket** *Allonemobius maculatus*
These little crickets have a very high, fast, pulsing, and burry trill, sounding like "ti-ti-ti-ti. . . ."

49. **Tinkling Ground Cricket** *Allonemobius tinnulus*
They are named for their call, which consists of a steady train of "tink-tink-tink." The tinks are faster and closer together in warm weather and may resemble the trill of a slowly calling Allard's Ground Cricket. In Tinkling Ground Cricket, however, you can always make out the individual "tink." In Allard's, the notes run together to create a trill. Bear in mind, though, a slow calling Allard's can make separating them very difficult.

50. **Allard's Ground Cricket** *Allonemobius allardi*
Their call is a high, sustained trill broken by brief pauses.

51. **Striped Ground Cricket** *Allonemobius fasciatus*
Listen for a high, burry "chit . . . chit . . . chit. . . ." The call is indistinguishable from that of the Southern Ground Cricket, which is best separated by range. The northernmost range of Southern Ground Cricket is southern New Jersey. The southernmost range of Striped Ground Cricket is northern Virginia.

52. **Southern Ground Cricket** *Allonemobius socius*
Southern Ground Crickets are very closely related to the preceding Striped Ground Crickets. They are best separated by where they are found. If the cricket is north of southern New Jersey, it's likely to be a Striped Ground Cricket. If it's south of northern Virginia, it's likely to be a Southern Ground Cricket. Anywhere in between, and it's anyone's guess.
    Their call is a high, burry "chit . . . chit . . . chit. . . ."

53. **Cuban Ground Cricket** *Neonemobius cubensis*
The call, given day and night, is a high-pitched trill.

54. **Sphagnum Ground Cricket** *Neonemobius palustris*
Their stridulation produce a series of sustained, high, feeble trills. When combined with other singing males in the bog, the trill sounds continuous. They are only found in open sphagnum bogs.

55. **Carolina Ground Cricket** *Eunemobius carolinus*
There is little doubt you've heard this one. It produces a continuous "riiiiiiiiiiii-iiiiiiiiiiiiiiiiiiiiiiiiiiiiiiiiiiiiiiiiiii." The "i" in "ri" is a soft vowel, as in the word "rigor," a good word to associate with this cricket, as it is one of the first to begin calling in spring and one of the last to call it a season in late fall.

56. **Jumping Bush Cricket** *Orocharis saltator*
Listen for a series of short, rich trills coming from the trees.

57. **Forest Scaly Cricket** *Cycloptilum trigonipalpum*
The call is a quiet, buzzy "zeeet-zeeet-zeeet . . . zeeet-zeeeet. . . ." There are several second pauses between each two-to-five-"zeeeet" sequence.

58. **Two-spotted Tree Cricket** *Neoxabea bipunctata*
The stridulation produces a buzzy, dry trill broken with short pauses. Sometimes the trill is continuous.

59. **Narrow-winged Tree Cricket** *Oecanthus niveus*
The song is a soft, pulsing trill, sounding like a ringing phone. The call lasts for two to six seconds with the pause lasting nearly as long. Refer to the field guide for separating this call from the pulsing calls of other tree crickets.

60. **Four-spotted Tree Cricket** *Oecanthus quadripunctatus*
Listen for a rich, high, continuous trill. Black-horned, Pine, and Fast-calling Tree Crickets have similar calls. You can refer to the field guide for more clues on telling them apart.

61. **Black-horned Tree Cricket** *Oecanthus nigricornis*
Their call is a rich, high, continuous trill.

62. **Fast-calling Tree Cricket** *Oecanthus celerinictus*
    Its song is a continuous, high, very rapid trill, sometimes interrupted by brief pauses. While the song can be confused with that of other tree crickets, if you are hearing it north of New Jersey, you can most likely rule out this species.
63. **Pine Tree Cricket** *Oecanthus pini*
    The song is a rich, high, continuous trill. While other tree crickets can produce a similar trill, if it's coming from a conifer, there's a good chance it's this species.
64. **Davis's Tree Cricket** *Oecanthus exclamationis*
    Their call is a rich, high trill of uneven lengths, broken by uneven pauses.
65. **Broad-winged Tree Cricket** *Oecanthus latipennis*
    Latipennis has the loudest call of the tree crickets, which is likely due to its very broad wings. The call is a rich, continuous trill.
66. **Snowy Tree Cricket** *Oecanthus fultoni*
    The song consists of a series of rich, evenly spaced chirps; faster and higher in pitch on warm nights; slower and lower in pitch on colder nights.
67. **Handsome Trig** *Phyllopalpus pulchellus*
    Listen for a high, rapid, "skritchy," irregular trill of short pulses.
68. **Say's Trig** *Anaxipha exigua*
    The call is a high, sustained, "breathy" trill.
69. **Columbian Trig** *Cyrtoxipha columbiana*
    The song consists of a series of high, steady, short, tinkling trills. The trills and spaces between trills are about equal in length. They are often synchronized with the trills of other males.

Author's note: Recordings 2, 5, 6, 11, 13, 18, 22, 23, 24, 28, 35, 36, 38, 46, 48, 53, and 67 were generously provided by the Walker Tape Library, located online at Thomas J. Walker's Web site "Singing Insects of North America" (http://buzz.ifas.ufl.edu/index.htm).

GLOSSARY

Apical. Tip, or farthest from the base.

Basal. At or near the base.

Basal antenna segment. The lowermost, often widest, segment of the antennae.

Cerci. Plural form of *cercus*, one of the paired projections extending from the tip of the abdomen. The varying shapes of the cerci are often used to identify species, particularly in the subfamily Conocephalinae (meadow katydids).

Cone. Elongated area extending from the top of the head.

Coniferous. Cone-bearing plants, often called evergreens.

Dactyl. Digging claw on the front leg of a mole cricket.

Deciduous. Pertaining to trees that shed their leaves.

Decurved. Bowing up toward the dorsal surface or edge.

Dorsal. The upper surface area or edge.

Dorsolateral. The area, often sharply or bluntly angled, between the dorsal (top) and lateral (side) surfaces.

Femora. Plural for *femur*, the section of leg between the body and tibia—the "thigh."

Genera. Plural for *genus*.

Genus. Part of the two-word naming system (binomial) of an organism. The genus name precedes the species name. Example: In *Scudderia furcata*, the genus is *Scudderia*.

Herbaceous. A plant bearing leaves and a stem that die at the end of the growing season.

Hind wings. Also called the inner wings, the pair of wings beneath the tegmina used for flight. Sometimes they are reduced or absent. Not all insects with hind wings can fly.

Lateral. Pertaining to the side.

Ovipositor. The elongated structure extending from the female's abdomen used to deposit eggs. The act of laying eggs is called ovipositing.

Palp or palpus. Single form of *palpi* or *palps*. The elongated, paired structures emanating from the lower area of an insect's face. They are mainly sensory organs.

Pronotal disc. The dorsal surface of the pronotum.

Pronotum. The plate that wraps around the top and sides of the thorax.

Sonogram. Pictorial representation of sounds, usually in a linear sequence similar to a bar code.

Spermatophore. A gelatinous packet containing sperm produced by the male, which is attached to the female's reproductive opening.

Spine. A fixed (unmovable) sharp, slender projection most often found on the tibiae.

Spur. A movable spinelike projection on the hind tibia.

Stridulary area/field/organ. The area on the tegmina that contains the file and scraper for producing sound. It is located on the basal and dorsal section of the tegmina.

Stridulation. The act of engaging the file and scraper in the stridulary area to produce a sound.

Subgenital plate. The lower plate of the last abdominal segment. In some males it is elongated, and curves up toward the supra-anal plate.

Supra-anal plate. The upper (supra) plate of the last abdominal segment. In the *Scudderia* (bush katydids), the differing size and shape of the supra-anal plate helps to distinguish species.

Tarsi. Plural for *tarsus*, they are the segmented part of the leg, or "feet," attached to the tibiae.

Taxonomist. A biologist who specializes in the classification of organisms into groups on the basis of their structure, origin, and behavior.

Tegmina. Plural for *tegmen*. The forewings, also known as upper or outer wings. They are usually thickened and distinctively veined. In katydids they are mostly opaque, green or brown, and wrap around the abdomen. In crickets, they are transparent to translucent, sometimes opaque, and usually rest flat on the abdomen.

Terminal. Farthest from the base; can be synonymous with *apex*.

Tibiae. Plural for *tibia*, the length of leg between the femur and the tarsus.

Tympanum. The hearing organ, or eardrum, located on the front tibiae of most katydids and crickets.

INDEX OF SCIENTIFIC NAMES

INDEX OF COMMON NAMES